youth football coaching

sessions
volume 2

tony charles and stuart rook

youth football coaching

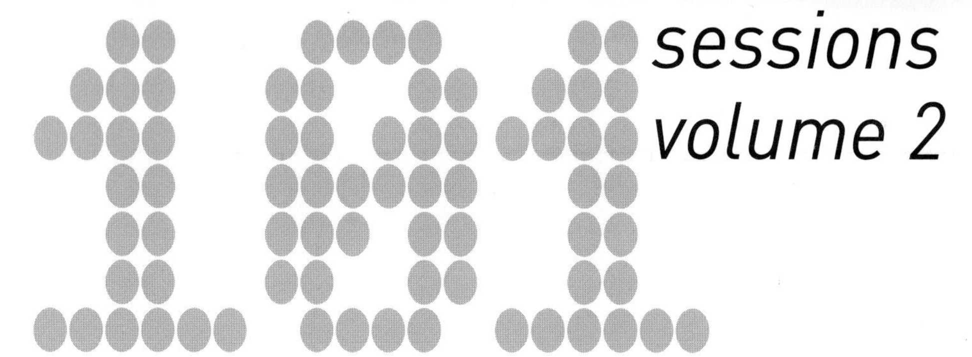

sessions volume 2

BLOOMSBURY
LONDON • OXFORD • NEW YORK • NEW DELHI • SYDNEY

Bloomsbury Sport
An imprint of Bloomsbury Publishing Plc

50 Bedford Square
London
WC1B 3DP
UK

1385 Broadway
New York
NY 10018
USA

www.bloomsbury.com

First published in 2017

Illustrations by Mark Silver

British Library Cataloguing-in-Publication Data
A catalogue record for this book is available from the British Library.

Library of Congress Cataloguing-in-Publication data has been applied for.

ISBN: Paperback: 9781472935786
ePub: 9781472935793
ePDF: 9781472935809

2 4 6 8 10 9 7 5 3 1

Typeset in DIN by Deanta Global Publishing Services, Chennai, India
Printed and bound in Great Britain by CPI Group (UK) Ltd, Croydon CR0 4YY

CONTENTS

FOREWORD

Football coaches need to have a vast range of resources to enable them to deliver outstanding coaching sessions. Whether you are a teacher or a coach, the commitment to effective and excellent delivery in your role in order to ensure that the young players you work with are able to succeed and progress is paramount.

I believe that in *101 Youth Football Coaching Sessions Volume 2*, Tony Charles and Stuart Rook have created a unique approach to session planning and coaching by offering an extensive range of coaching topics, which ensures children of all ages can participate and enjoy football regardless of their level of ability, as every game is fun and inclusive.

Additionally, you can combine a number of warm ups, games and exercises to create a unique coaching session tailored entirely to the requirements of your players. This can be achieved with ease by following the numbers at the bottom of each page, which relates to another game with a similar topic.

The intention of *101 Youth Football Coaching Sessions Volume 2* is to provide coaches with a single point of access to a variety of different coaching sessions. Whether coaching at grass roots or at the top level in professional football, all coaches need to ensure that their sessions are both fun, safe and informative, and Tony Charles and Stuart Rook certainly deliver this inclusive message.

Dean Holdsworth
Ex-professional footballer and A Licence coach

INTRODUCTION

The primary aim of this book is to help youth football coaches and players get the most out of each and every coaching sessions they deliver and attend. Our belief is that developing players improve their understanding and technique when they are enjoying themselves. By drawing on over three decades of experience, and with a little help from our coaches, we have created a second volume of 101 fun, informative and challenging coaching sessions, designed to give players the maximum time with the football and to help them to improve their football ability.

We have designed each session to be as inclusive as possible, with as many players working with a ball, or in small groups, as often as is viable, which will vary based on the focus of the specific technique for each game. This is in order to try to move away from old-fashioned line drills, where the players are standing and waiting for a turn and therefore may only touch a football once every few minutes. From our experience, the more involved each player is and the more enjoyment the session brings, the less likely they are to be disruptive or become disengaged from the session. Increasing the frequency of each player's touches of the ball will also help in their overall development.

The sessions

With the exception of the warm-ups, at the end of each session you will find a series of numbers – these are session numbers and relate to other games within the book. We have carefully selected games that we feel work well with others to create a complete football coaching session. Warm-ups can be applied to any session and what we have suggested is simply a guide for you to work from and develop into your own coaching sessions, as we feel a coach should be adaptable and, above all, imaginative.

Within the sessions we have also suggested where the coach should position him or herself. This is to help the players get the most out of the session as the coach will be able to view and correct the technique of players during the session and be able to deliver coaching points and progressions effectively. It will also ensure that the coach can survey the entire area and see everything that is happening on a wider scale, particularly during small-sided games. Being able to see the 'bigger picture' is an essential coaching skill and incorporating this into your sessions will help players develop into more complete footballers.

The position of the coach suggested in each session means the coach will not be interfering with the play, allowing it and therefore the session to flow freely, while maintaining control from a broader viewpoint.

The timing for each session will depend on the age group and length of your session. For example, an hour long after-school club might consist of a warm-up game (5–10 minutes), a fun football game (15–20 minutes), then a conditioned small-sided practice (10–15 minutes), which would then naturally develop into a practice match at the end.

For a 90-minute or two-hour session, you might want to spend more time on a specific technique or on two different techniques, incorporating three or four different fun football games – or you may wish to spend more time on the small-sided game conditioned practices. In this instance, a longer warm-up would benefit the players by preparing them for a longer session. The warm-up games can also be used as a cool down at the end of the session.

Club coaches may well be able to identify the area of their team they feel needs specific improvement, and should design a session plan with that goal in mind. Being able to spot certain strengths and weaknesses of a team or a player and then planning how to improve on those weaknesses or make best use of the strengths could be the difference between a good team and a great team.

We believe that to be a good coach you need to let your personality come across in your sessions. Each page is a guide for you to use: feel free to adapt any game to allow it to work best for you.

Finally, our biggest hope is that this book will inspire coaches, teachers and parents to develop fresh, entertaining and informative sessions and that they will always be positive, show encouragement and provide examples of fair play. Keep up the good work and keep laying the foundations for the football futures of young players.

Happy coaching!

ABOUT FOUNDATION SPORTS

Our work with schools sees us deliver sports coaching sessions to children of all ages and abilities from a mixture of backgrounds. Foundation Sports works closely with schools to up-skill their workforce to ensure the teaching staff in primary schools across London are confident and competent to deliver effective PE lessons. Foundation Sports allows all schools to be able to access professional coaching. We have created one of the country's leading community schemes by delivering educational and sports-related projects in schools. We also target those (particularly the young) who are perceived as socially excluded from mainstream provision ensuring that we initiate and develop accessible and affordable projects.

If you require further information about Foundation Sports please visit: www.foundationsports.com

ACKNOWLEDGEMENTS

We would like to thank all the coaches from Foundation Sports for their valuable input, particularly Leon Othen.

Session 11 – Contributed by Noah Lown
Session 22 – contributed by John Mejicks
Session 34 – contributed by Keeley Makinson-Wyatt
Session 40 – contributed by Steve Shepheard
Session 72 – contributed by David Greene

WARMING UP

Warming up is one of the most important aspects of your coaching session. It is vital that your players are warmed up properly in order to maximise their performance and reduce the risk of injury. A warm-up also helps the players to concentrate on the session ahead.

All of our warm-up sessions can be used at the beginning of any coaching session as they are inclusive and are not restricted to one specific football technique. Particular emphasis is given to the importance of developing and mastering the basic physical literacy skills of agility, balance, co-ordination and speed, along with spatial awareness.

session 1 cone commands

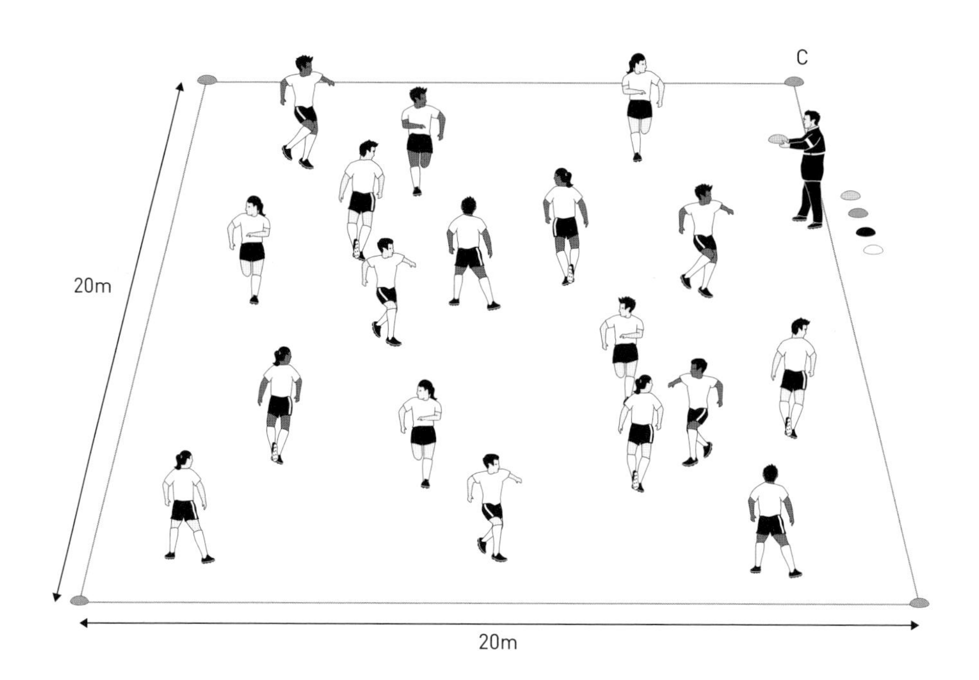

Organisation: Set out a 20 x 20m area

Equipment: Bibs, marker cones, footballs.

Description: Players move around inside the area. Without speaking, the coach holds up one cone at a time with each colour having a simple movement instruction to follow.

Examples of instructions: Green cone = go (move around the area); red cone = stop (stand still); yellow cone = get ready to go (jog on the spot); blue cone = move around the area backwards; white cone = players lay down on their back on the floor (if it's not wet or muddy).

Key coaching points: Encourage lots of movement. Spatial awareness. Observational skills.

Progression: Coach makes up more colour commands. Add a ball per player, so players can dribble around the area while watching out for each command to then perform.

session 2 cops & robbers

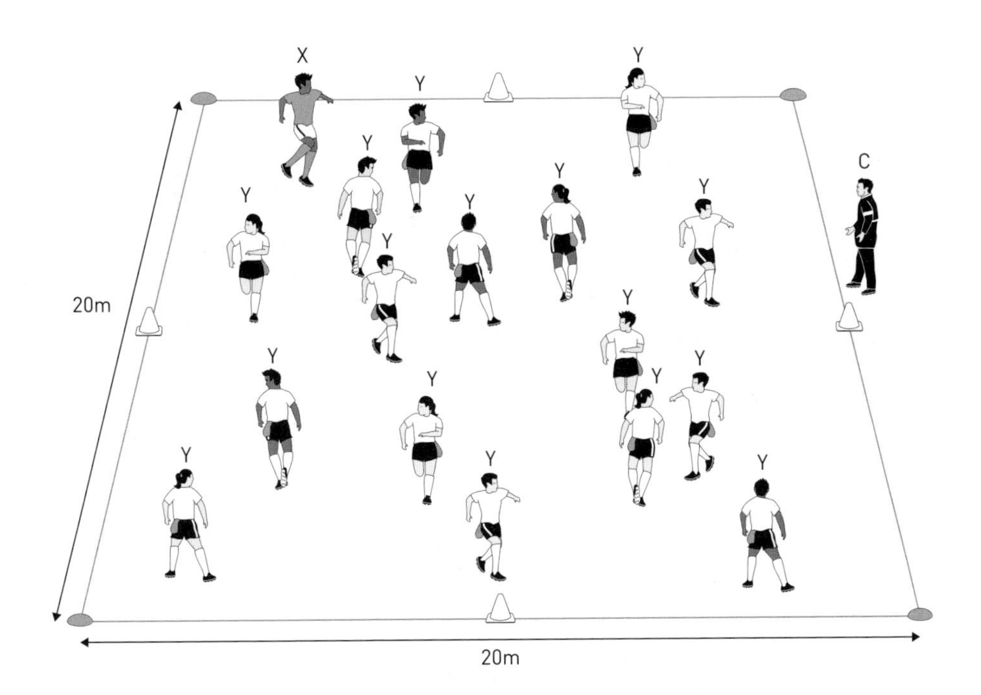

Organisation: Set out a 20 x 20m area with four traffic cones placed in the middle of each side. Select one player to be the catcher (X). All other players (Y) take a bib each and place it into the waistband of their shorts, hanging down like a tail.

Equipment: Traffic cones, bibs.

Description: The cop (X) tries to catch the robbers (Y) by chasing them around the area trying to pull out their bibs. Once the bib is pulled out, the robber has been caught and has to 'go to jail' and is out of the game. If a robber has their hand on any of the four traffic cones, they are in the 'safe house' and cannot be caught, but they may only stay in the safe house for a maximum of five seconds.

Key coaching points: Look around to make sure you don't get caught, and see the 'safe houses'. When a cop chases you, turn to face them so that it's harder for them to pull out the bib. Move in as many different directions as you can.

Progression: Add extra cops. Reduce the amount of 'safe houses'. When a robber gets caught they become a cop.

session 3 noughts & crosses

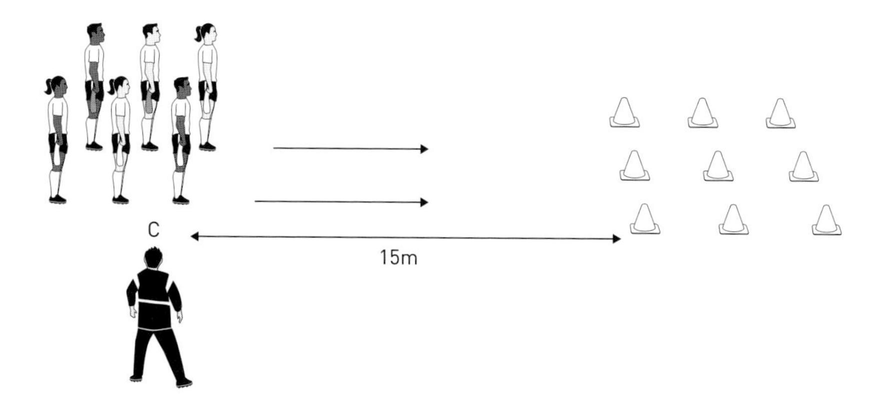

Organisation: Set out nine hoops, mats, quoits or cones in a 3 x 3 grid. Organise the players into teams of three, holding a bib each and stationed 15m away from the grid. Each team needs to have a different coloured bib, i.e. red v blue.

Equipment: Marker cones, bibs.

Description: This is played as a 3 v 3 game of noughts and crosses. One player from each team runs out and places their bib on top of a cone then returns to their team. The next player then runs out and places their bib on top of a cone, attempting to make a line or block the opposition from making a line. If all three bibs from each team are placed into the grid but there is no winner, the players keep rotating until one team successfully makes a line of three bibs in a row.

Key coaching points: Move quickly to gain an advantage over the other team. Decision making – think about trying to make a line of three or blocking your opponents from making a line of three.

Progression: Advance the game into a 4 x 4 grid with a line of four required to win the game.

session 4 knock knock

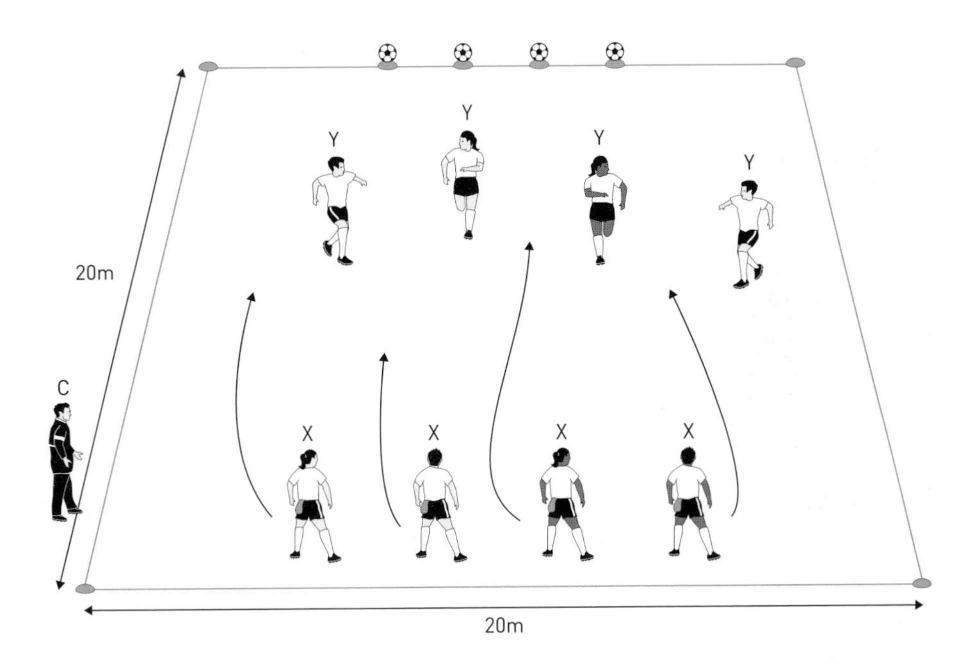

Organisation: Set out a 20 x 20m area and balance four footballs on top of small cones at one end. Select four defenders (Y) who start in the middle of the area, and four attackers (X) who start on the opposite baseline and each have a bib placed it into the waistband of their shorts, hanging down like a tail.

Equipment: Marker cones, bibs, footballs.

Description: The X players attempt to evade the defenders (Y), make it to the other end of the area and knock off one of the four footballs. If the defender is able to catch the attacker by pulling out their tail, they swap roles and start again. If the attacker manages to knock a ball off, they are awarded one point, then reset the ball and have another go.

Key coaching points: Move quickly to lose your defender. Spatial awareness.

Progressions: Play 1 v 1 as a relay in teams. Move the four footballs to the other sides of the square to change the angle of attack and defence.

session 5 action ball

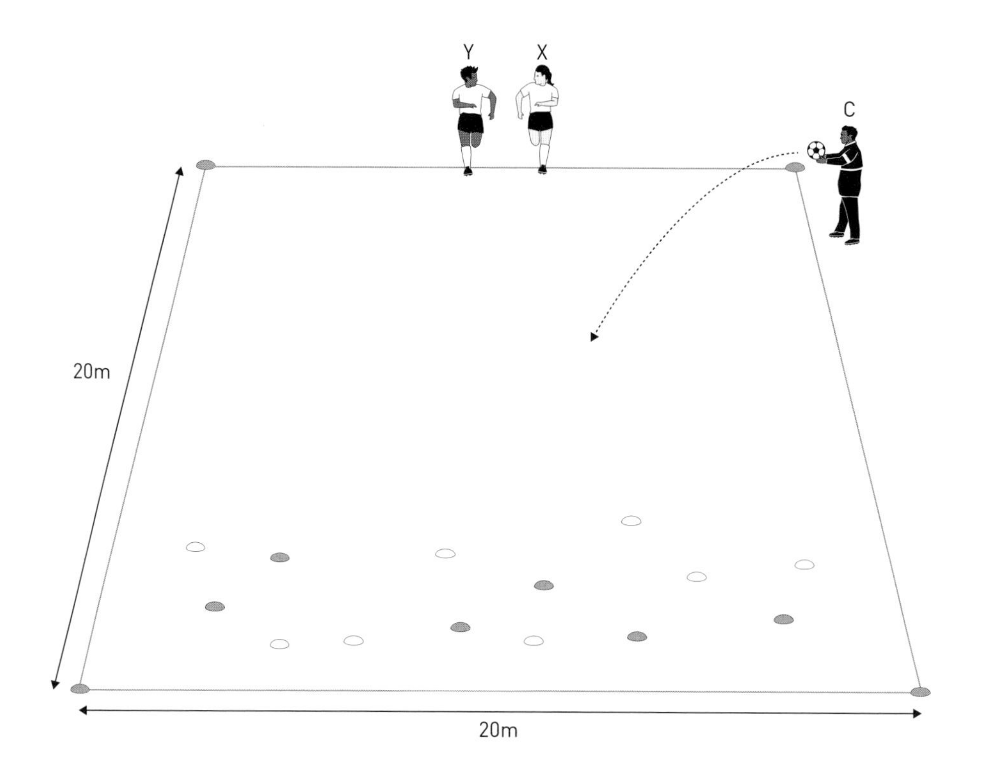

Organisation: Set out a 20 x 20m area with a large number of different coloured small cones scattered at one end. Set up players into two teams (X and Y), with players competing 1 v 1 inside the area.

Equipment: Marker cones, bibs, football.

Description: With one player from each team starting in the centre on the baseline, the coach calls out a colour and then throws the ball into the area. The players then race to the opposite end to touch the cone of that colour and then to the ball. Whichever player is first to collect the ball wins a point for their team.

Key coaching points: React quickly to get to the cone and back to the ball. Spatial awareness.

Progressions: Play 2 v 2 in pairs, the coach throws three footballs into the area. The pair that gets two balls wins the point. Develop into a passing practice with players having to dribble the ball back to the coach.

session 6 square in a square in a square

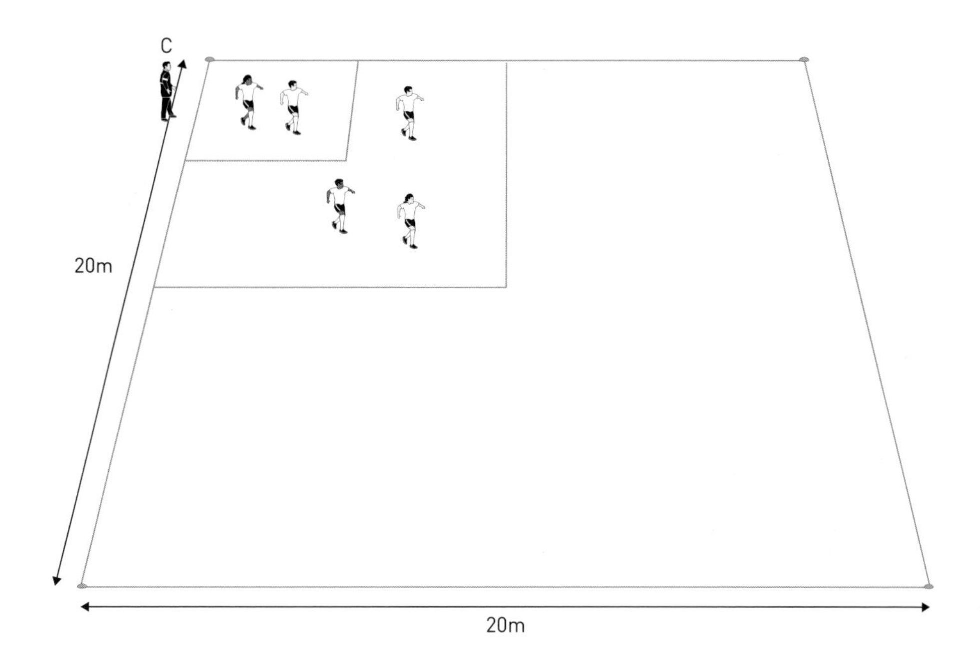

Organisation: Set out a 20 x 20m (big) square with a 10 x 10m (medium) inside, and then a 5 x 5m (small) square inside that.

Equipment: Marker cones, bibs.

Description: Start with all players inside the 5 x 5m square. When the coach calls either big, medium or small, the players all have to move into the correct size square whilst trying to avoid bumping onto any other players.

Key coaching points: Spatial awareness. Quick reactions to different instructions.

Progressions: Add a fun forfeit for any players that bump into each other. Add in different movements such as jumping, skipping, hopping and crawling.

session 7 circle command

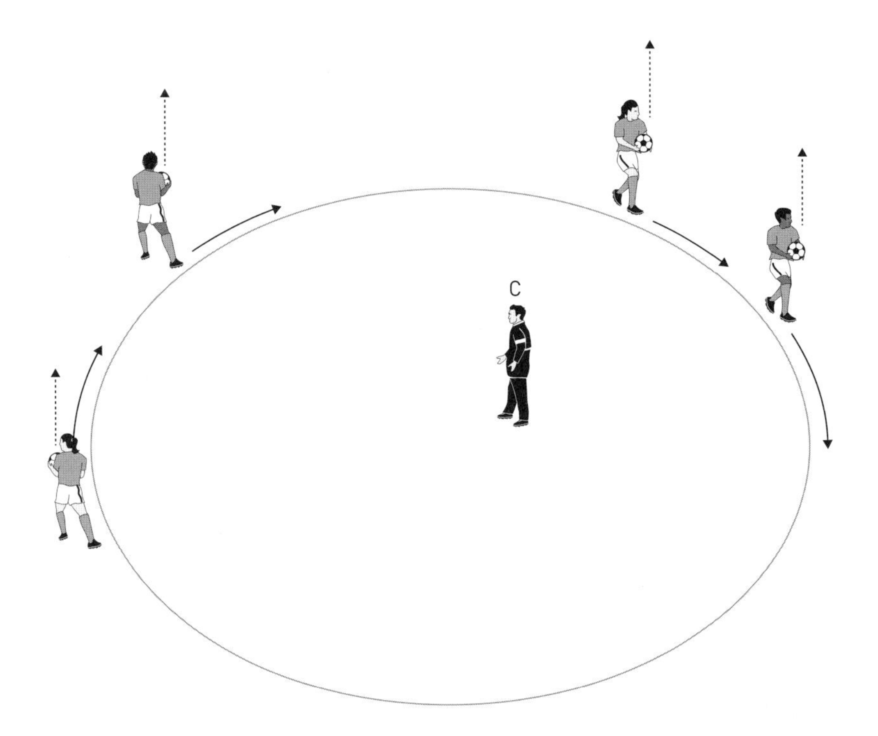

Organisation: The players are set up in a circle (the centre circle of a football pitch works well).

Equipment: Marker cones, footballs, cones.

Description: The players are evenly spaced out around the circle and move in the same direction. On the coach's command, the players stop and change direction. Introduce a football for each player. The players move around the circle perimeter throwing their football in the air and catching it. On the coach's command players throw their ball high in the air and then run and catch the ball that the person in front of them threw.

Key coaching points: Spatial awareness. Control of football.

Progressions: Dribble the football around the circle perimeter. On the coach's command, turn with the football. On the coach's command, stop the ball and move forwards to dribble with the next football in front.

session 8 animal tag

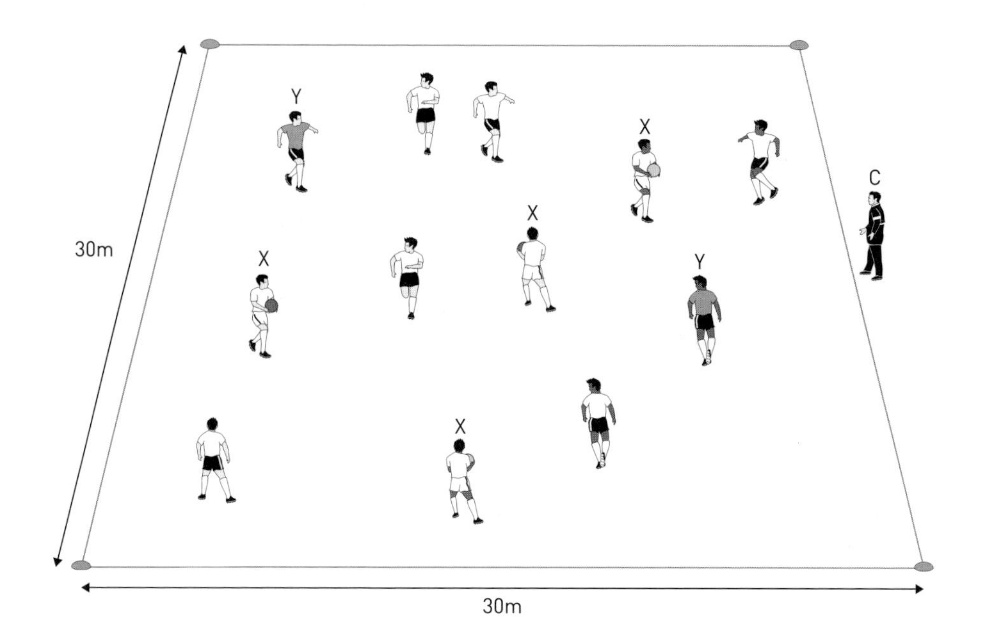

Organisation: Set out a 30 x 30m area. Four players are chosen to be 'animals' (X) and two are chosen to be 'officers' (Y) while the other players run around and try to avoid getting caught. Two of the 'animals' hold the green balls or 'freeze balls' and two hold the red balls or 'dance balls'. The two 'officers' wear bibs.

Equipment: Marker cones, 2 bibs, 2 red and 2 green balls.

Description: The officers must 'unfreeze' the players that have been caught by the freeze and dance animals. Whenever the freeze animals move towards the other players, they have to freeze in order to prevent getting caught and whenever they see a dance animal coming towards them, they need to dance to prevent getting caught. If a player is caught, they need to freeze in an animal pose until the officers come and unfreeze them by tagging them.

Key coaching points: Spatial awareness. Good dance moves.

Progression: Increase the number of balls and animals and/or officers.

session 9 secret doctor

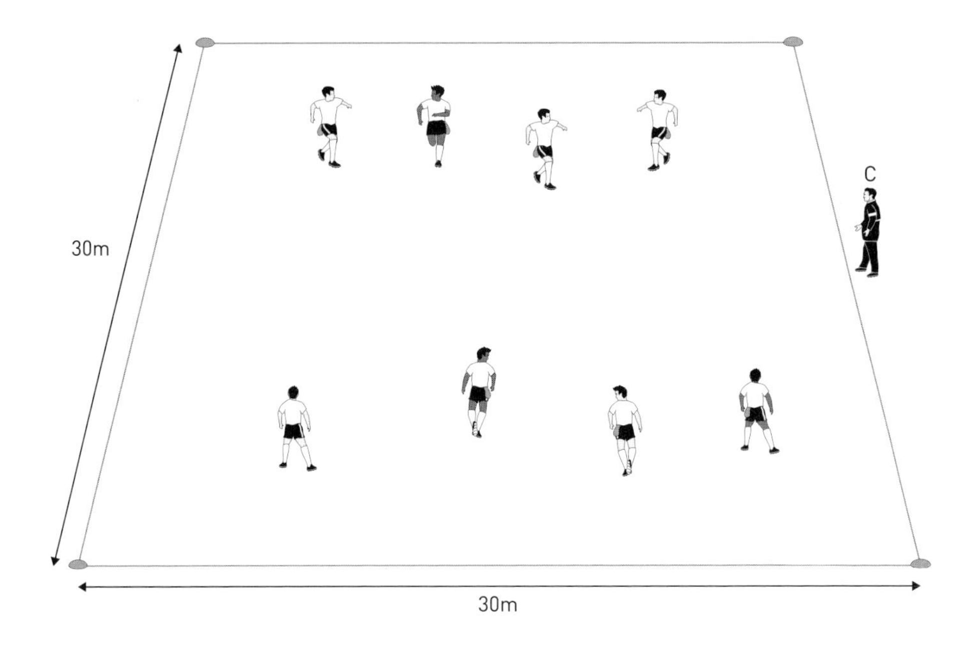

Organisation: Set out a 30 x 30m area for all players.

Equipment: Marker cones, bibs.

Description: Split the class or group into two equal teams. The players each place a bib in their shorts, hanging down like a tail, and each team needs to nominate a 'Secret Doctor'. The teams then play tag against each other by pulling out the tail from a member of the opposition. If the tagged player is given a high five by the Secret Doctor they are back in the game. The team with the most players left untagged after three minutes wins.

Key coaching points: Spatial awareness. Communication.

Progressions: Overload the teams. Add a time limit

session 10 battlefield

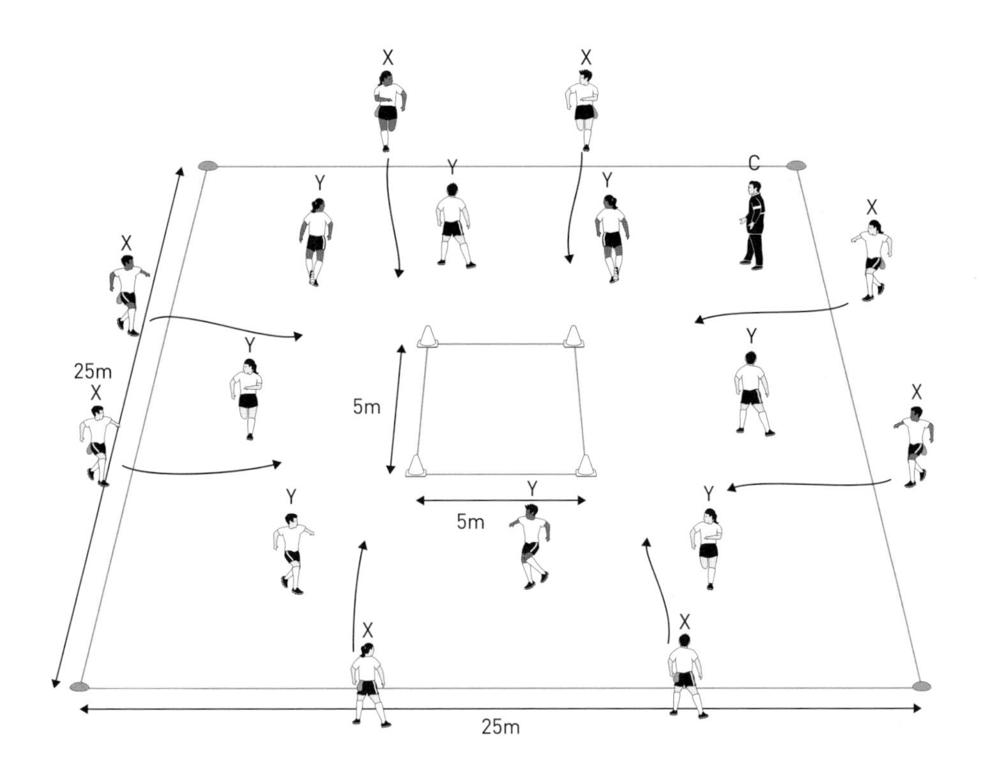

Organisation: Set out a 25 x 25m area with a 5 x 5m square in the centre. Organise the players into two equal teams, with one team (X) attacking, standing outside the main area and the other team (Y) defending, standing in the 'battlefield', i.e. inside the area, but outside the small square in the centre. The attacking team (X) have bibs tucked into their shorts.

Equipment: Marker cones, traffic cones, bibs.

Description: The attacking team members (X) aim to move from outside the area, through the battlefield and into the centre square without having their bib pulled out by the defenders (Y). They can start at any point outside the area and can retreat back behind the line to be safe. If they make it into the centre, they get one point for their team and wait there until the game is over. Any defending player can pull out the bib of any attacking player. Once all of the attacking team are either in the centre square or out of the game (bib pulled out), the teams swap roles and attempt to score more points than their opponents.

Key coaching points: Look around to make sure you get through the battlefield without getting caught. Work as a team to catch the attackers. Move in as many different directions as you can.

Progressions: Add a time limit. Defenders have to hold a bib between them and work in pairs to catch the attackers. Award points to individual defenders for each time they catch an attacker to add a competitive element between defenders.

session 11 foot, foot, ball

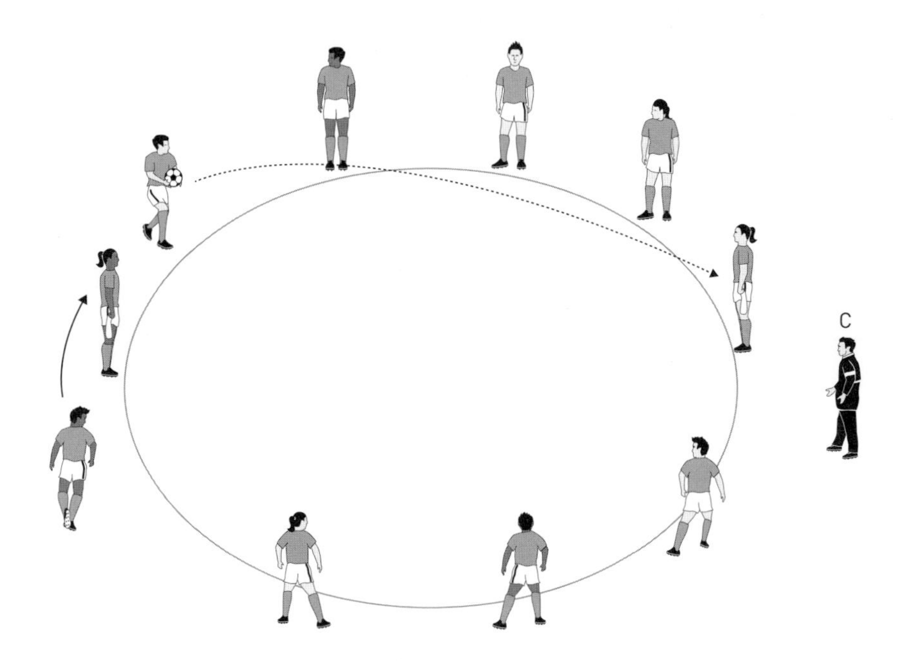

Organisation: Organise players into a circle with one ball.

Equipment: Marker cones, bibs, ball.

Description: The game starts with the players in the circle throwing a ball to each other. One player (X) is selected to move around the outside of the circle and, similarly to a classic game of 'duck, duck, goose', taps each player on the shoulder, but instead says 'foot, foot ... ball'. Whomever X touches and says 'ball' to chases X around the circle for a full lap trying to tag them before they take their space in the circle and catch the football as it is thrown to them when they arrive. The chaser then becomes the next selecting player.

Key coaching points: Movement. Spatial awareness. Observational skills.

Progressions: Pass the football using feet. Add a second football. Two-touch passing.

session 12 copy cat

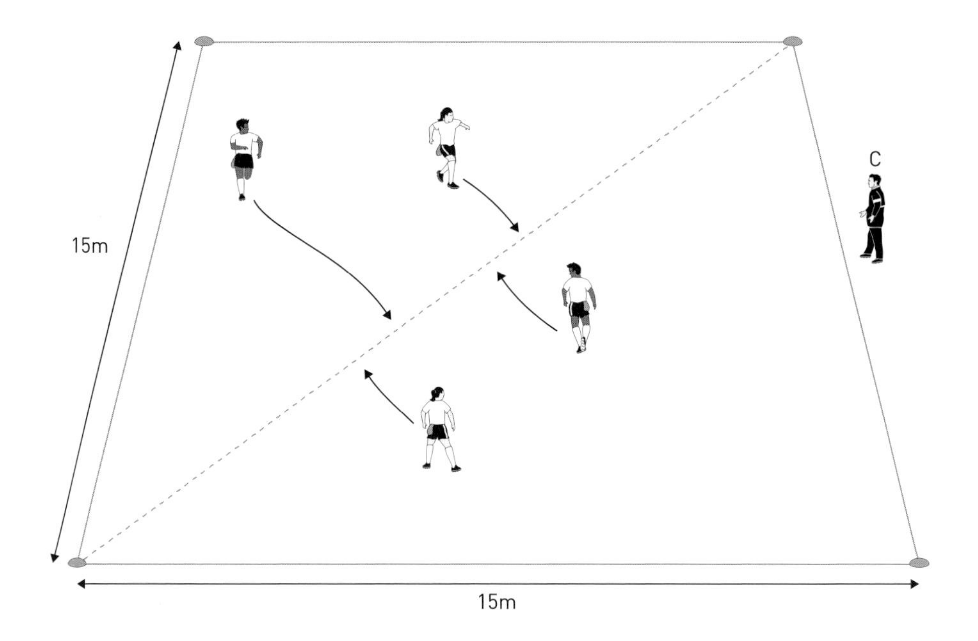

Organisation: Set out a 15 x 15m area with a line running diagonally across, dividing the square into 2 triangles. Place two players into each of the triangles. Each player should have a bib placed into the waistband of their shorts, hanging down like a tail.

Equipment: Marker cones, bibs, ball.

Description: Staying inside the triangle, the players compete 1 v 1 to try to steal their opponent's bib. Play best of three wins and then rotate the pairs so that they play against someone new.

Key coaching points: Movement. Speed and change of direction. Reactions.

Progressions: Add a time limit to the game. Play 2 v 2.

session 13 crocodiles

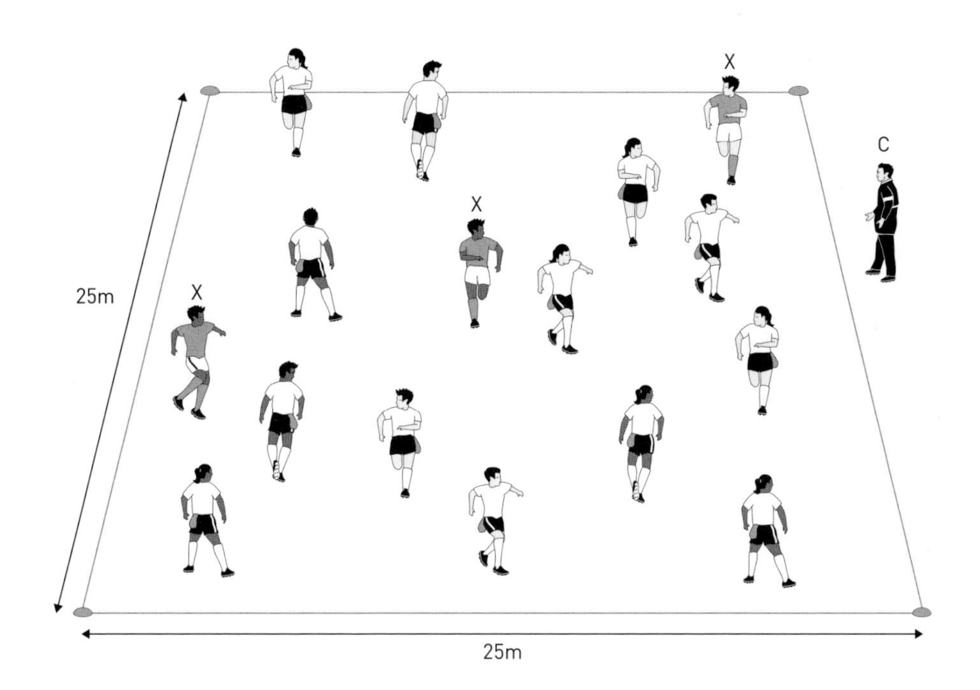

Organisation: Set out a 25 x 25m area. Select three players to be 'crocodiles' (X), with the rest of the players spread around the area with a bib each placed it into the waistband of their shorts, hanging down like a tail.

Equipment: Marker cones, bibs.

Description: The players move around the area attempting to avoid getting caught by the crocodiles. If they are caught (bib pulled out), they join up with the crocodile by holding one end of the bib each and then attempt to catch more players together.

Key coaching points: Movement. Speed and change of direction. Spatial awareness.

Progressions: Add extra crocodiles. Give each player a ball to dribble.

session 14 lizard's tail

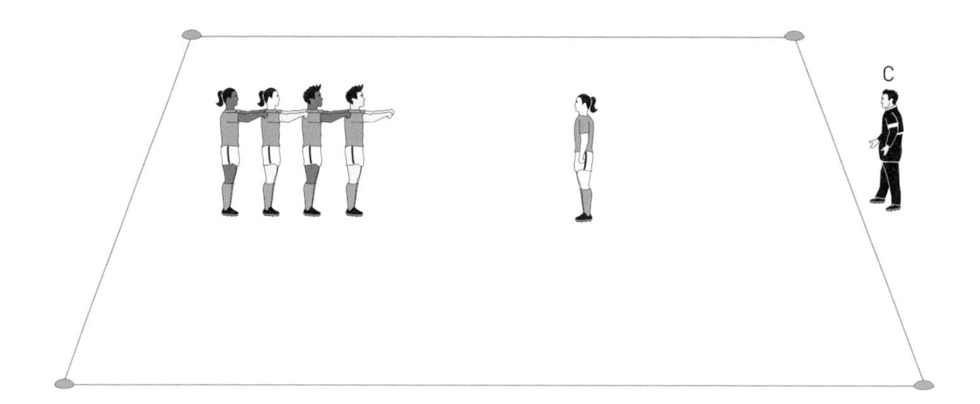

Organisation: Players are in groups of four or five. All players except one stand in a single file line facing in the same direction with their hands on the shoulders of the person in front. They form the lizard's body with the player at the back being the tail. The single player stands facing the others – they are the lizard's head.

Equipment: Marker cones.

Description: On a command from the coach, the lizard's head tries to tag the lizard's tail. The body of the lizard tries to stop this from happening by moving back and forwards between the head and the tail. They must remain joined at all times. The first person in the line may not grab the lizard's head to stop them reaching the tail nor use their arms to obstruct the head. When the head tags the tail, the head joins the front of the line and the tail becomes the new head – start again. If a group is having difficulty tagging, they may just swap after a designated time.

Key coaching points: Spatial awareness. Movement. Teamwork.

Progression: The lizard's head stays on and has to chase the tail.

session 15 ball tag

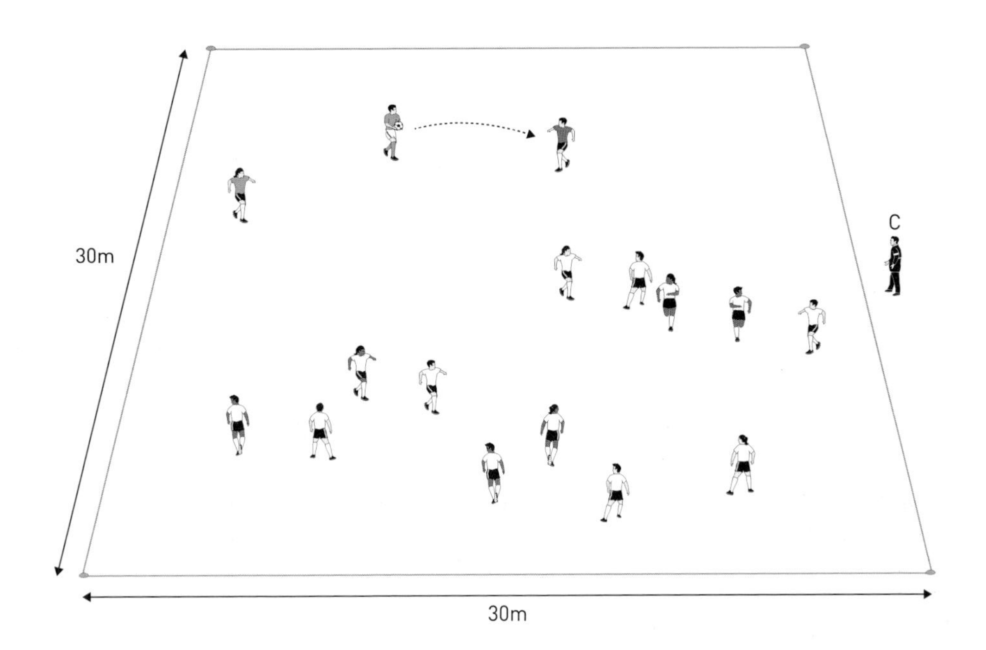

Organisation: Set out a 30 x 30m area for all players.

Equipment: Marker cones, bibs, football.

Description: Nominate 1–3 players to become 'taggers' and give them a bib so they can be identified. Tell the other players that they now have to dodge and evade the taggers otherwise they are out. Taggers move around with the ball, passing to each other. They can only tag whilst in possession with the ball (ball must touch the target). Explain that the ball cannot be thrown or kicked at the target during the game. The taggers have 1–2 mins to play the game.

Key coaching points: Spatial awareness.

Progressions: Increase the number of taggers. Increase the time to play the game.

session 16 mr men/little miss

Organisation: Set out a 30 x 30m area for all players.

Equipment: Marker cones.

Description: Explain to the players that they are now going to become the Mr Men or Little Miss characters. The coach then calls the name of a character and the players have to move like them:

Mr/ Little Miss Slow = move slowly; Mr/ Little Miss Rush = move fast; Mr/ Little Miss Jelly = shake your whole body; Mr/ Little Miss Muddle = walk backwards; Mr/ Little Miss Bounce = bounce; Mr/ Little Miss Small = crouch while moving; Mr/ Little Miss Strong = move, flexing your muscles; Mr/ Little Miss Tall = stretch up and move (good for stretching once the players' hearts are racing); Mr/ Little Miss Tickle = wave arms around in a crazy way; Mr/ Little Miss Happy = move around with big smiles on your face.

Key coaching points: Spatial awareness. Listening to the coach.

Progression: Introduce a football for each player to dribble at the same time.

session 17 team foxes & farmers

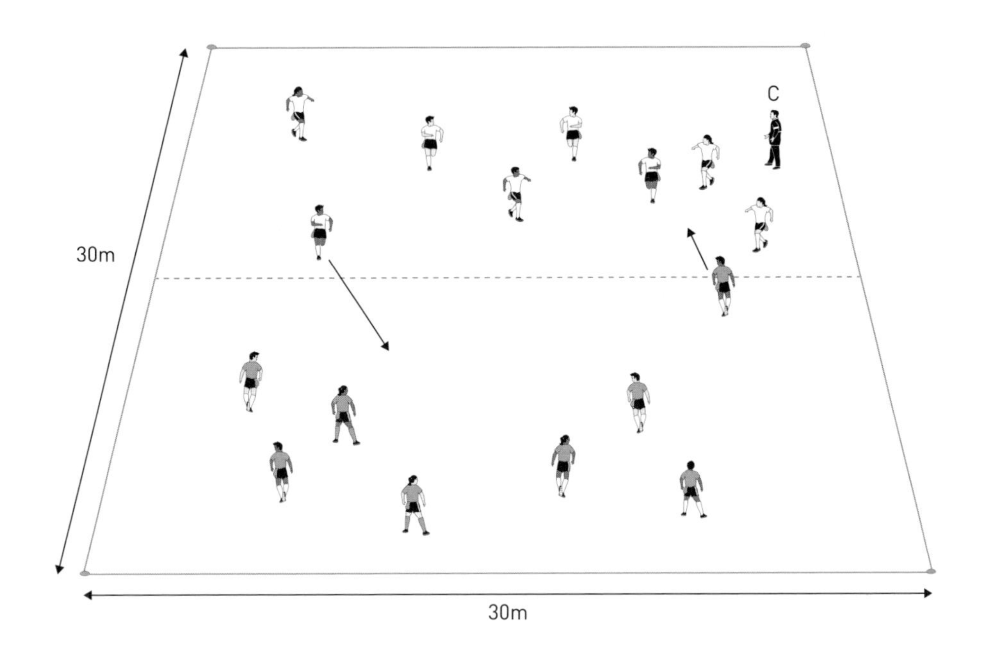

Organisation: Set out a 30 x 30m area for all players with a halfway line dividing the area into two equal-sized halves. All players have a bib each tucked into the waistband of their shorts, hanging down like a tail. Give each player a number and divide the players into two groups – the 'foxes' and the 'farmers'.

Equipment: Marker cones, bibs.

Description: The players move around their own half of the area. As the coach calls out two numbers from each team, those two players need to run into the opposite half of the area and attempt to pull out all the bibs of the opposition players. Once a bib is removed, that player is eliminated. The fastest pair to pull out all the bibs wins a point for their team. Play again with different numbers and keep score as you go.

Key coaching points: Spatial awareness. Movement. Teamwork.

Progressions: Increase the number of players allowed into the opposition half each time. Introduce a time limit.

session 18 circle exchange

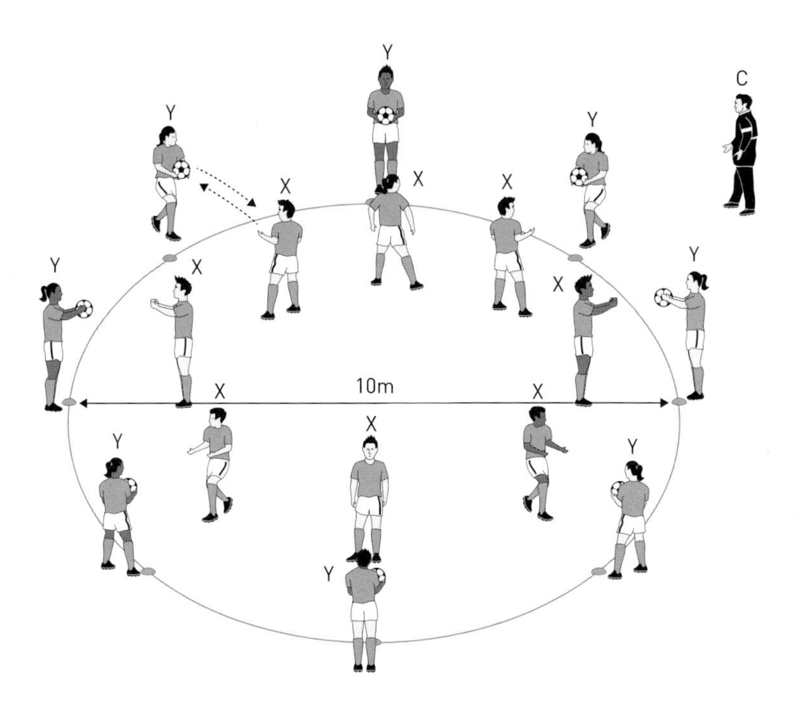

Organisation: Set out a circle 10 metres in diameter. Half of the players stand inside a circle, the other half are on the perimeter of the circle with a football each.

Equipment: Marker cones, footballs.

Description: The players (Y) are evenly spaced out around the perimeter of circle. The players (X) inside the circle move around creating space. On the coach's command, every X player moves towards a Y player and asks for the ball. The X player then receives the ball in their hands and throws it immediately back to the Y player.

Key coaching points: Spatial awareness. Communication. Control of your football.

Progressions: Return the ball with another body part. Control, then return the ball with another body part. Pass the ball to another Y player.

session 19 keeper command

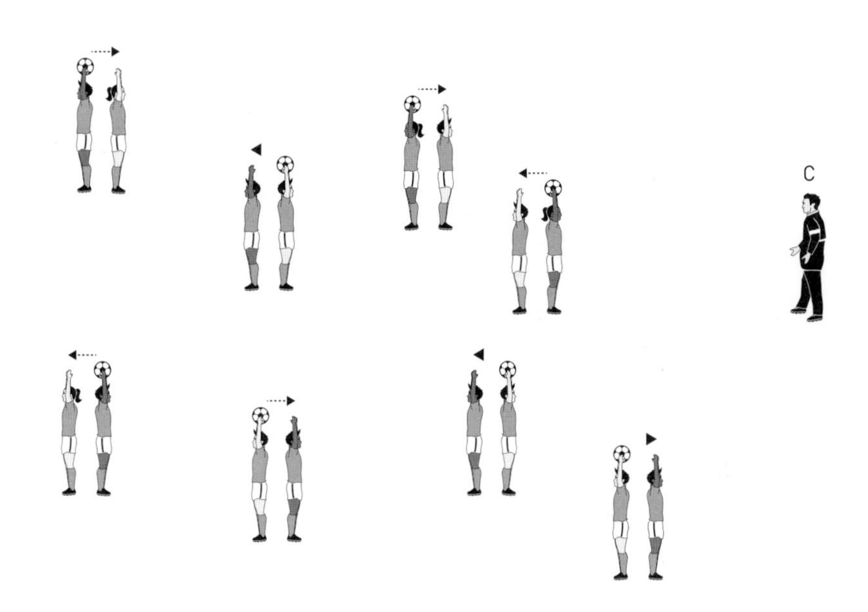

Organisation: Players have a football between two.

Equipment: Marker cones, footballs.

Description: On a command from the coach, the players work in pairs (X and Y) to perform several movements: Trunk twists = players stand back-to-back 1–2 metres apart. Player X rotates around from the trunk and passes the ball to their partner (Y), who has likewise rotated around. Under/over = players stand back-to-back 1–2 metres apart. Player X passes the ball over their head to Y who reaches back to collect the ball. Player Y then passes the ball through their legs to X who reaches through their own legs to collect the ball.

Key coaching points: Control of your football. Communication.

Progressions: Number of passes in a minute. Players pass the ball to each other using the correct catching technique. Players pass the ball to each other over a distance of around 10 metres using correct technique.

session 20 team knee tag

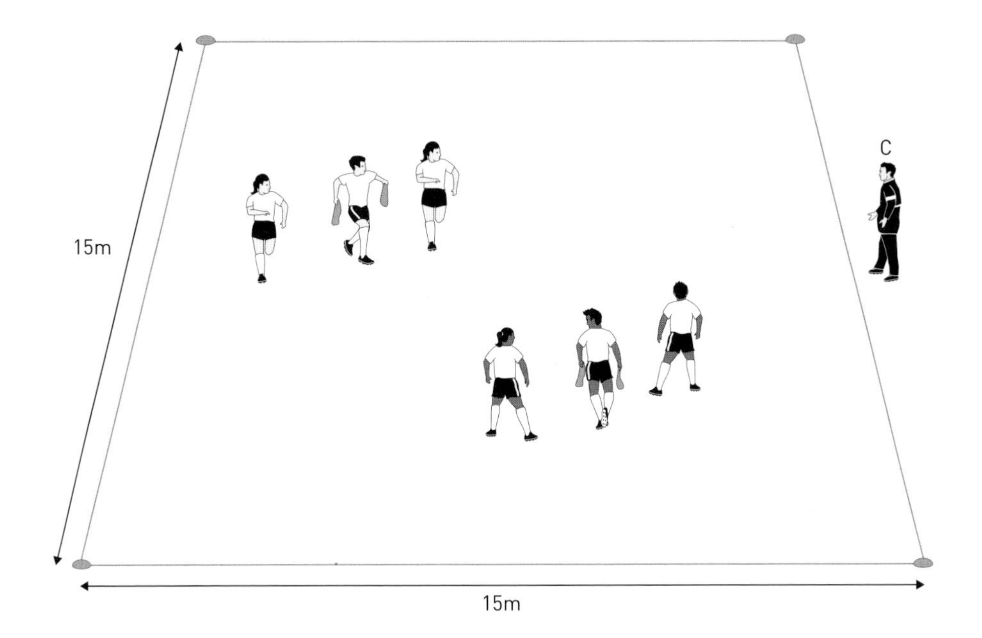

Organisation: Set out a 15 x 15m area. Organise players into teams of three holding two bibs between them with a player on each side and one in the middle.

Equipment: Marker cones, bibs, ball.

Description: The teams play facing each other and score a point by tagging a member of the other team on the knee. Teams must stay facing each other at all times.

Key coaching points: The two end players will be able to use their free hand to attempt a tag, but the middle player will be holding both bibs so needs to communicate. Movement. Teamwork.

Progressions: Increase the number of players in each team. Limit the game so that only the player in the middle is allowed to be tagged.

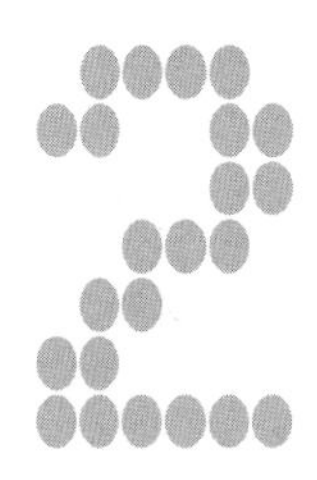

FUN FOOTBALL

In this section you will find games that range from very easy and simple techniques to more challenging practices for advanced players. These sessions are designed to be simple to execute and fun in practice for both coach and player.

The more basic games in this section serve as a great platform for players who are starting out in football, while the more advanced sessions are designed to put players to the test in order to develop as a player.

Regardless of the level of difficulty, the aim of each game is to engage the player's imagination and enthusiasm for football without focusing too heavily on technique – guided discovery over mundane line drills.

session 21 colour cone jumble

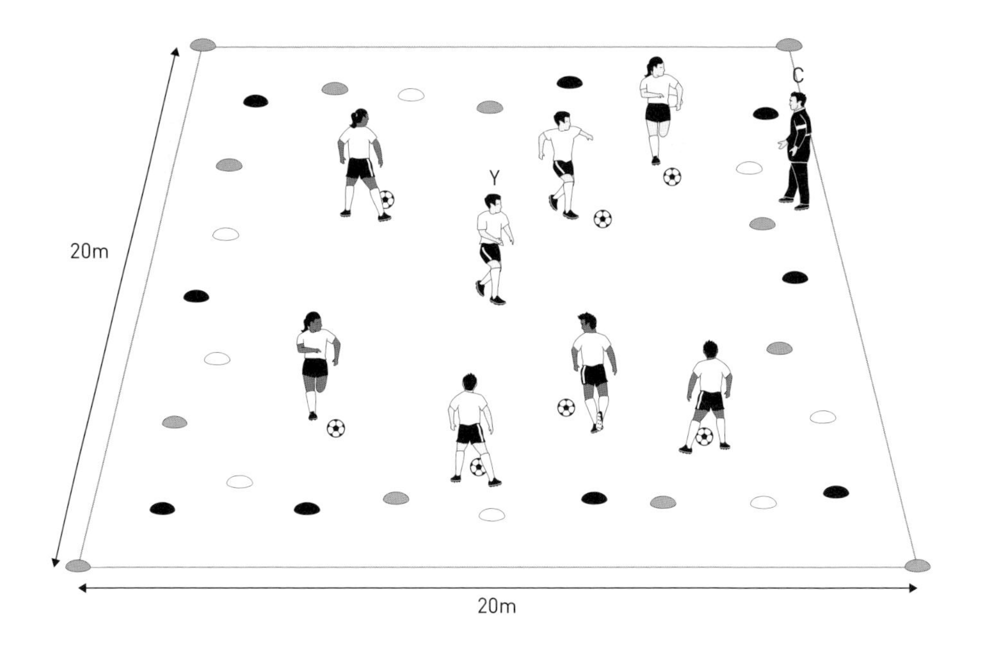

Organisation: Set out a 20 x 20m area with coloured cones in three different colours scattered around the edge of the area. Each player has a ball, except one player (Y) who is standing in the middle of the area without a ball.

Equipment: Marker cones in four colours, footballs.

Description: Players dribble the footballs around the area, while player Y moves without the ball. When the coach calls out a colour, the players leave their ball and race to touch a cone of that colour. They then have to try to recover any ball before the player without a ball (Y) 'steals' one.

Key coaching points: Keep the ball close to your feet when dribbling. React quickly to get to the coloured cone, and then get back to a ball. Head up and looking around for space when dribbling.

Progressions: Add extra 'stealing' (Y) players. Dribble the ball using left or right foot only. Reduce the amount of coloured cones.

››› 29 – 35 – 63 – 97

session 22 steal the ball

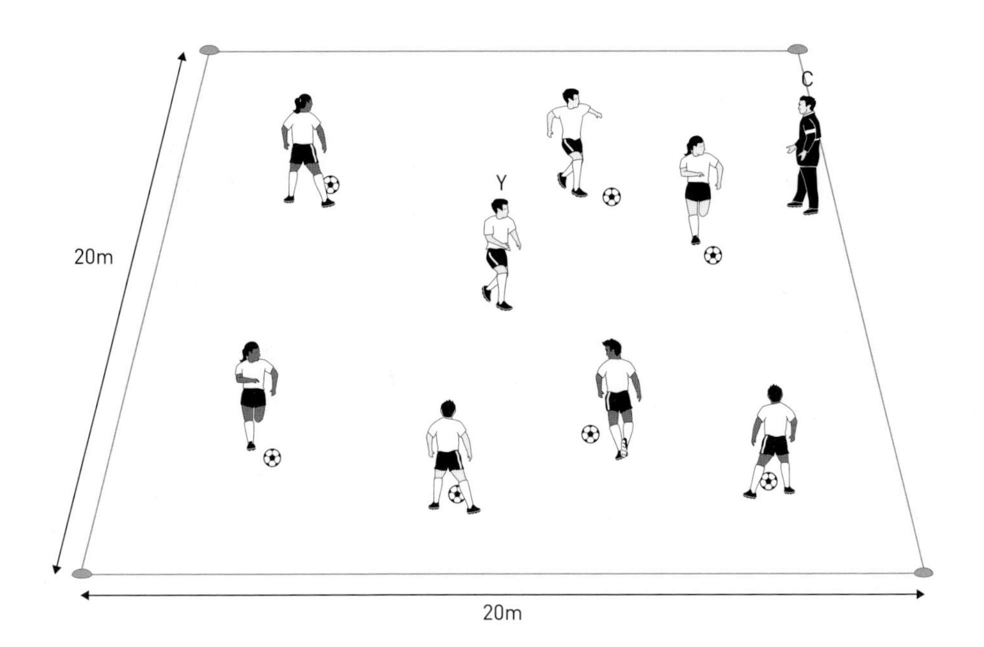

Organisation: Set out a 20 x 20m area. Each player has a ball, except one player (Y) who is standing in the middle of the area without a ball.

Equipment: Marker cones, footballs.

Description: The aim is for the player without the ball (Y) to move around the area and 'steal' one from a player with a ball. The player who steals the ball successfully gets to keep it and continues to dribble, leaving the player whose ball got stolen to then go and steal a ball from another player. Each game has a time limit. The player left without a ball when the time elapses performs a fun forfeit. If a player's ball is stolen, they cannot steal the ball straight back they must move on to another player.

Key coaching points: Keep your head up. React quickly to turn away from the player trying to steal. Once you have a ball, try to keep it close to your feet.

Progressions: Add extra 'stealing' players. Before starting each player is given five points. Each time they lose possession of the ball they lose a point and if they lose all of their points, they are out. Dribble the ball using left or right foot only.

››› 26 – 41 – 43 – 76

session 23 trio

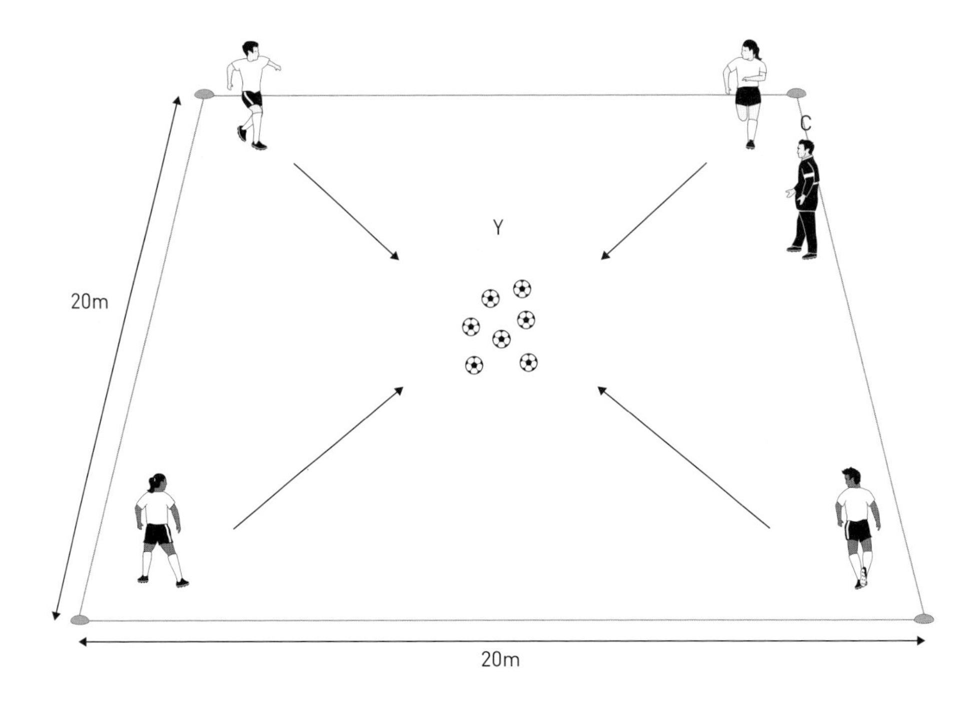

Organisation: Set out a 20 x 20m area, with one player in each corner and seven footballs in the middle of the square.

Equipment: Marker cones, balls.

Description: When the coach shouts go, the four players race to collect the footballs from the centre of the square and dribble them back to their corner. Once the footballs have all gone from the middle they may steal the balls from each other's corners, the first player to collect three footballs in their own corner is the winner.

Key coaching points: Keep your head up, looking around for opponents and their footballs. Once you have a ball, keep the ball close to your feet. Quick and sharp turns out of each corner.

Progressions: Dribble using left or right foot only. Use nine balls, the first to collect four is the winner. Play in pairs, taking alternate turns to collect a ball.

››› 32 – 54 – 64 - 99

session 24 danger squares

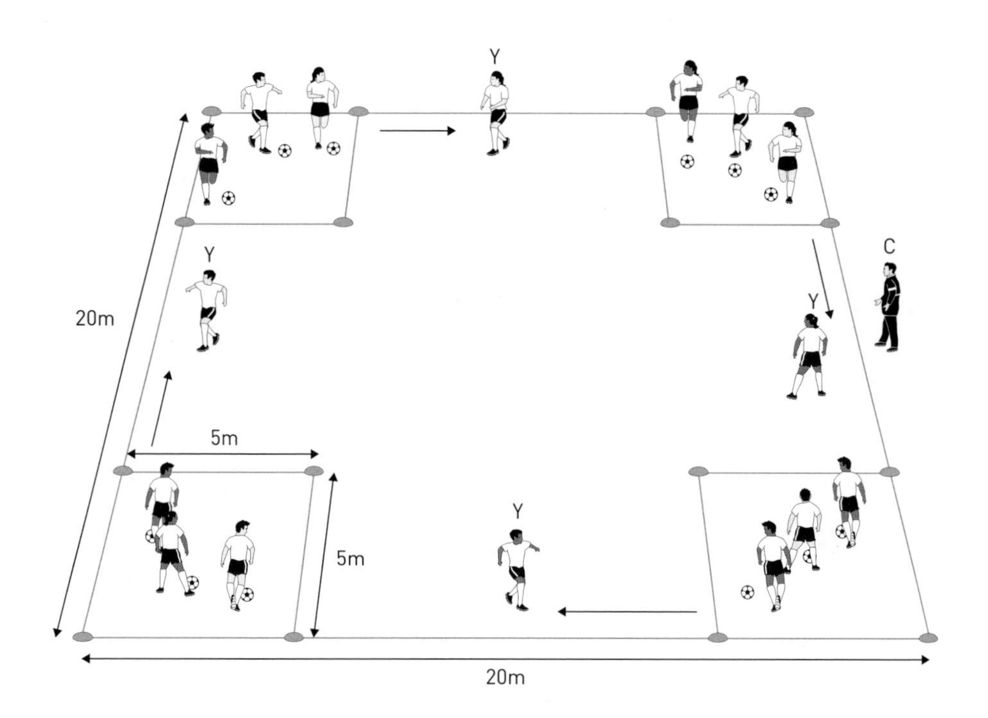

Organisation: Set out a 20 x 20m area with four 5 x 5m squares in each corner. Players are separated into teams of three and placed in each corner square. One defending player (Y) is placed halfway between each square.

Equipment: Marker cones, balls.

Description: Players dribble their ball around in the corner squares, in and out of spaces without making contact with one another. As the coach shouts 'Go', the players have to travel in a clockwise direction to the next square, without getting tackled by the defender in the middle (Y).

Key coaching points: Keep your head up, looking around for opponents and their footballs. Once you have a ball, keep the ball close to your feet. Quick and sharp turns out of each corner.

Progressions: Award points to defenders for each time they steal a ball to add a competitive element. If a player loses possession of their ball, they swap with the defender. Allow players to move in any direction when the coach calls 'Go'.

››› 40 – 41 – 65 – 82

session 25 triple 1 v 1

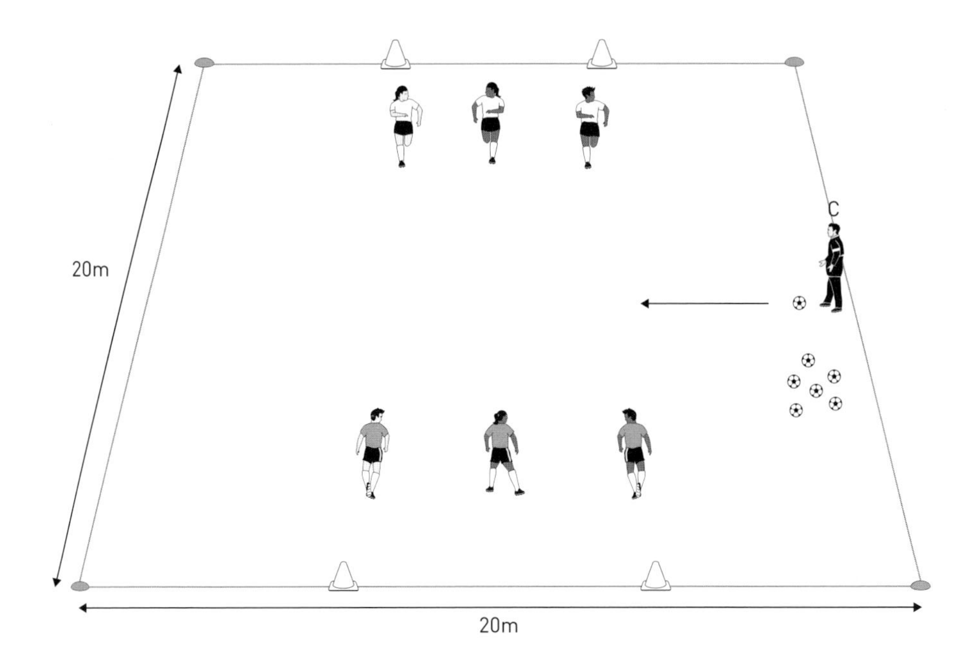

Organisation: Set out a 20 x 20m area, with two small goals set up on either side of the baseline. Organise players into two teams of three, set up in pairs as a 1 v 1 at the opposite end of the area. The coach stands between the two goals with some footballs ready to be played in.

Equipment: Marker cones, traffic cones, balls.

Description: The coach plays a football into the area to each of the pairs who play 1 v 1 inside the area. The aim is for one player to beat their opponent and score into either of the two goals to win a point for their team. If the ball leaves the field of play before a goal is scored, that game is a draw, and the players reset. Rotate pairs after each game so they play against a different opponent each time.

Key coaching points: Keep your head up, looking around for opponents and their footballs. Use your dribbling skills to beat your defender. Get low and side on when defending.

Progressions: Players have to stop the ball on the line inside the goal to score a point. Once a goal is scored or the ball leaves the field of play, those two players may now help out their teammates creating a 2 v 2 or 3 v 3. Add a goalkeeper to each goal.

››› 28 – 40 – 61 – 89

session 26 dr. football

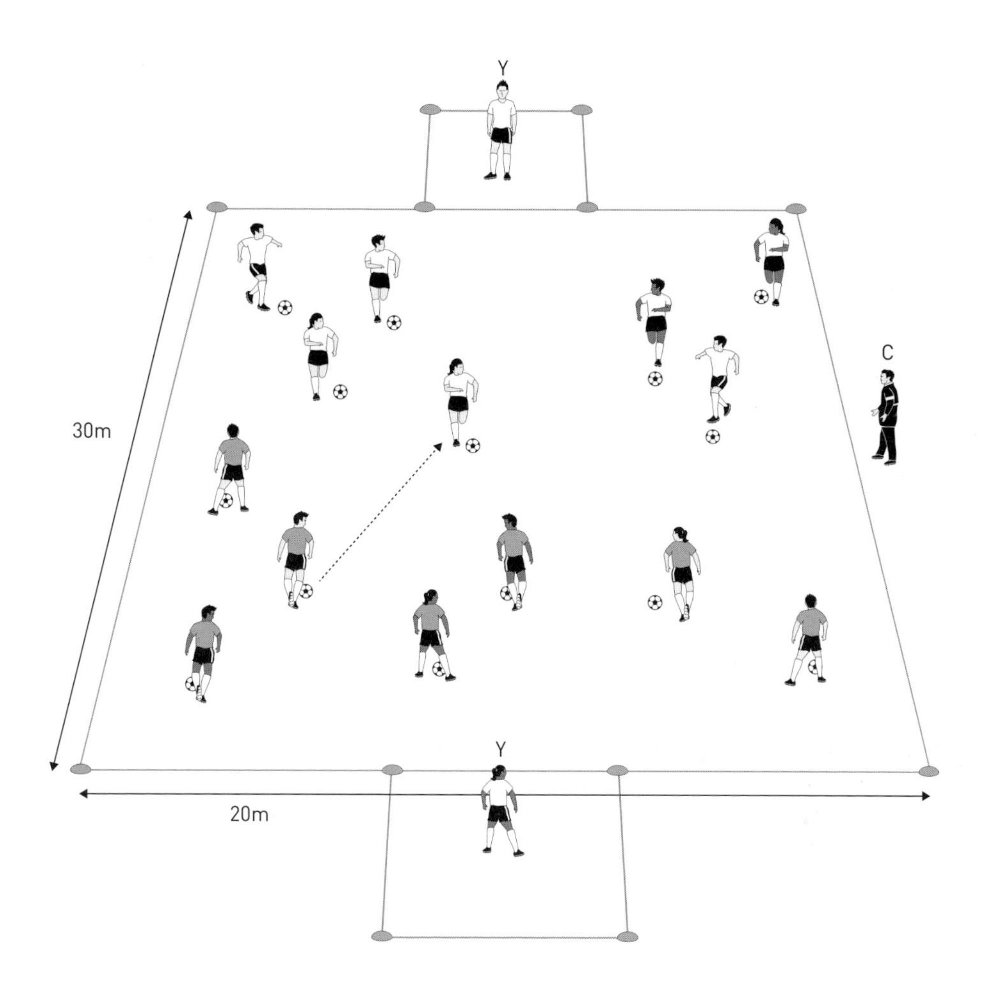

Organisation: Mark out a 20 x 30m area with a smaller square at each end. Organise the players into two even teams with different bibs. One player from each team (Y) is stationed inside one of the smaller squares – they are the 'doctor'. All players need a football, except the player inside the small square.

Equipment: Marker cones, footballs, bibs.

Description: The players from each team dribble their ball around the area, and try to eliminate their opponents by passing their football and hitting them below the knee. If a player is eliminated, they have to go down on one knee and are out of the game, but if they call their doctor to come and give them a high-five, they are back in. To win the game, you need to eliminate the opponent's doctor while they are outside of their square, but if they are in their square they are safe.

Key coaching points: Keep your head up, looking around for opponents and their footballs. Keep your ball close to your feet when dribbling. Use the inside of your foot to pass the ball accurately and eliminate your opponent.

Progressions: Allow each team to have two doctors. Remove the 'safe square' to make it harder for the doctors. Give each doctor a football so that all players can eliminate each other.

››› 22 - 52 - 64 - 76

session 27 team pursuit

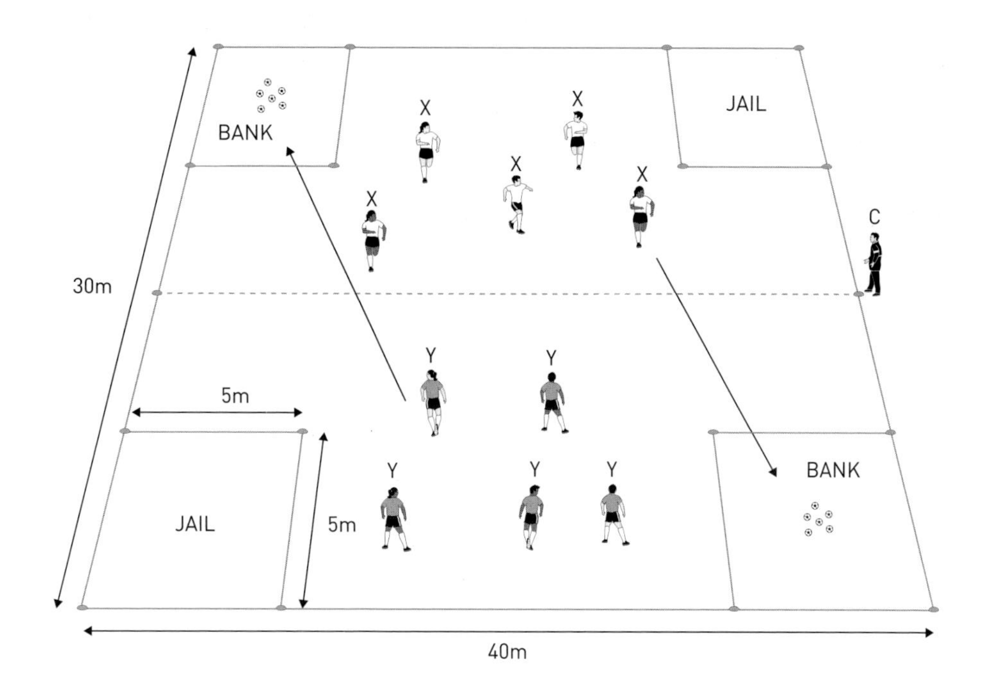

Organisation: Set out a 40 x 30m area. Divide the area into two halves with a centre line of cones. Mark out a 5 x 5m square in each of the four corners of the area, one square in each half is the 'jail' and the other is the 'bank'. Place an equal number of footballs in each team's bank and divide the players into two teams (X and Y)

Equipment: Marker cones, footballs, bibs.

Description: Each team aims to collect all the balls by invading the other team's half of the area, taking a football from their bank and dribbling it back to their own bank without getting tagged. Players are safe in their own half, but if a player is tagged while in the opponent's half, they must go directly to the opponents' jail. A player is released from jail only when a teammate crosses into the opposing half and high-five's them. The first team to collect all of the balls in their bank wins.

Key coaching points: Keep your head up, looking around for opponents and footballs. Keep your ball close to your feet when dribbling. Work as a team to try to collect balls, defend your own balls and release teammates from jail.

Progressions: Dribble using weaker foot only. Limit the amount of touches allowed to travel the ball from bank to bank, encouraging players to run with the ball rather than dribble. Allow teams to pass the ball to each other when stealing from the other team.

››› 37 – 39 – 65 – 86

session 28 multi goal 1 v 1

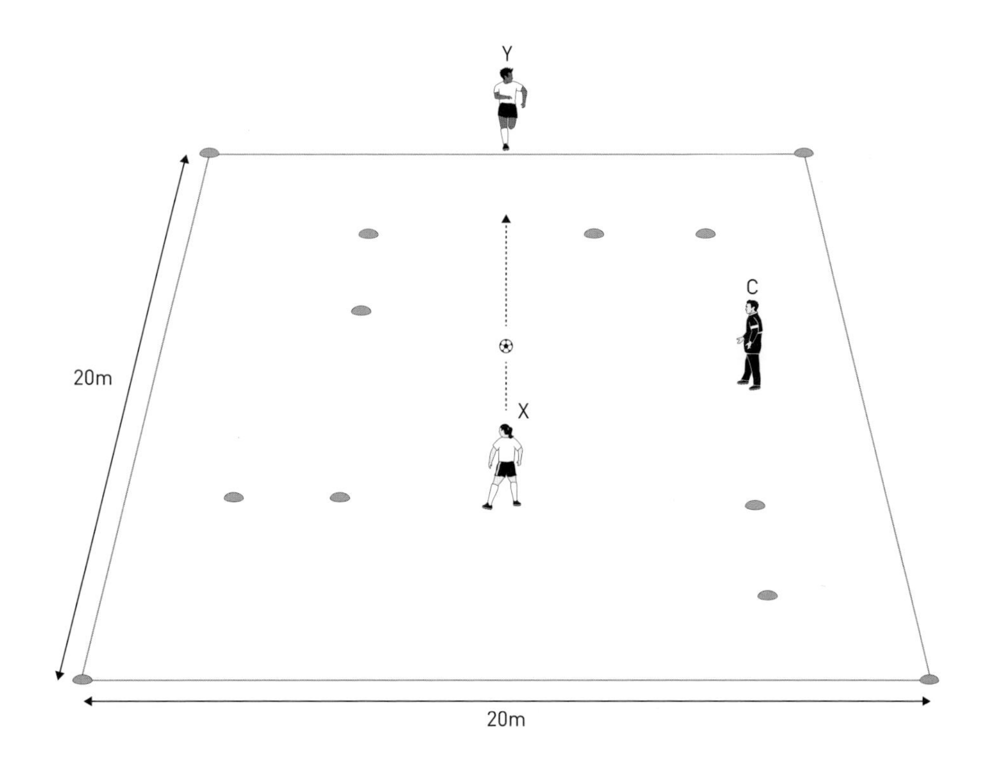

Organisation: Set out a 20 x 20m area with four small gates inside the area. Play 1 v 1 in pairs, with the defender (X) standing in the centre of the area and the attacker (Y) standing at the baseline.

Equipment: Marker cones, balls.

Description: The defender (X) starts with the ball and passes to (Y) on the baseline. The attacker then attempts to score a point by stopping the ball in the middle of any of the four small gates. If the defender clears the ball out to the area before a point is scored, then they win the point. Rotate after each round, the first player to reach ten points wins.

Key coaching points: Use your dribbling skills to beat the defender. Attack the space. Get low and side on to defend, and don't dive in!

Progressions: Add another attacker to create a 2 v 1. Add another attacker, and another defender to create a 2 v 2. If the defender wins the ball but it doesn't go out of play, they then become the attacker and try to score a bonus point.

››› 25 – 30 – 41 – 96

session 29 turnover

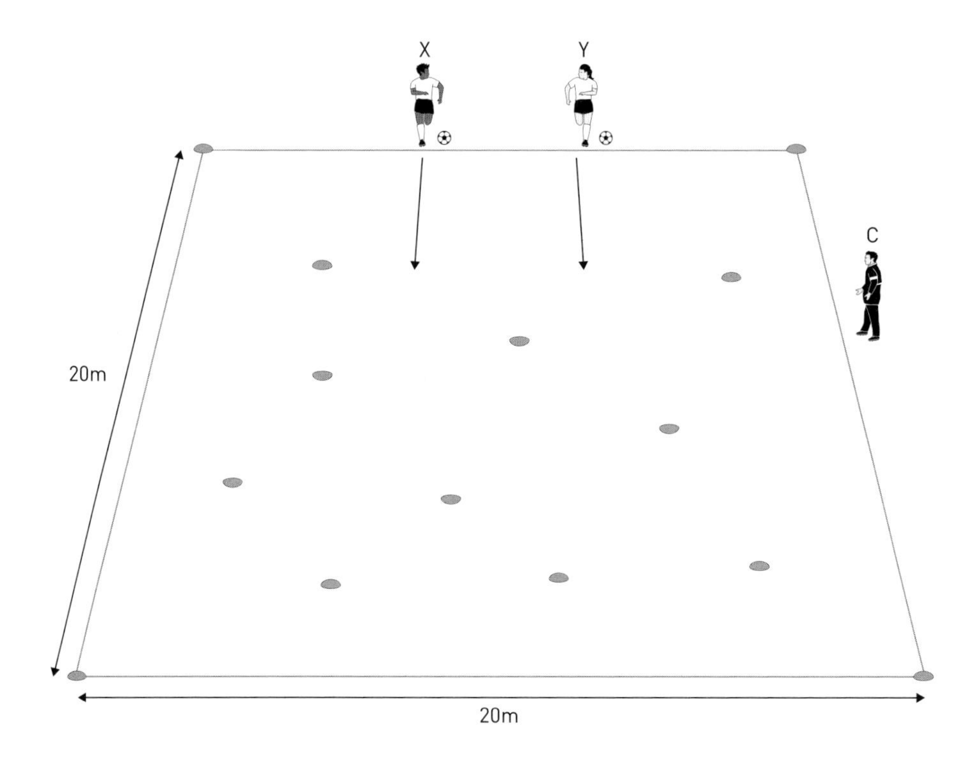

Organisation: Set out a 20 x 20m area with an equal number of domes (cones) and dishes (upside-down cones) scattered around the area. Set up two players on the baseline with a ball each.

Equipment: Marker cones, balls, bibs.

Description: One player is assigned the 'domes' and their opponent is assigned the 'dishes'. On 'Go', the players dribble around the area turning the cone over to either domes or dishes. Play for 30 seconds and whichever player has more domes or dishes at the end is the winner!

Key coaching points: Keep your head up, looking around for domes and dishes. Keep your ball close to your feet. Use quick, and sharp turns to change direction.

Progressions: Play 2 v 2 as a tag-team relay race. Play 2 v 2 with all players in the area with a ball each. Dribble using your weaker foot only.

››› 21 – 35 – 39 – 82

session 30 keep ball 1-2-3

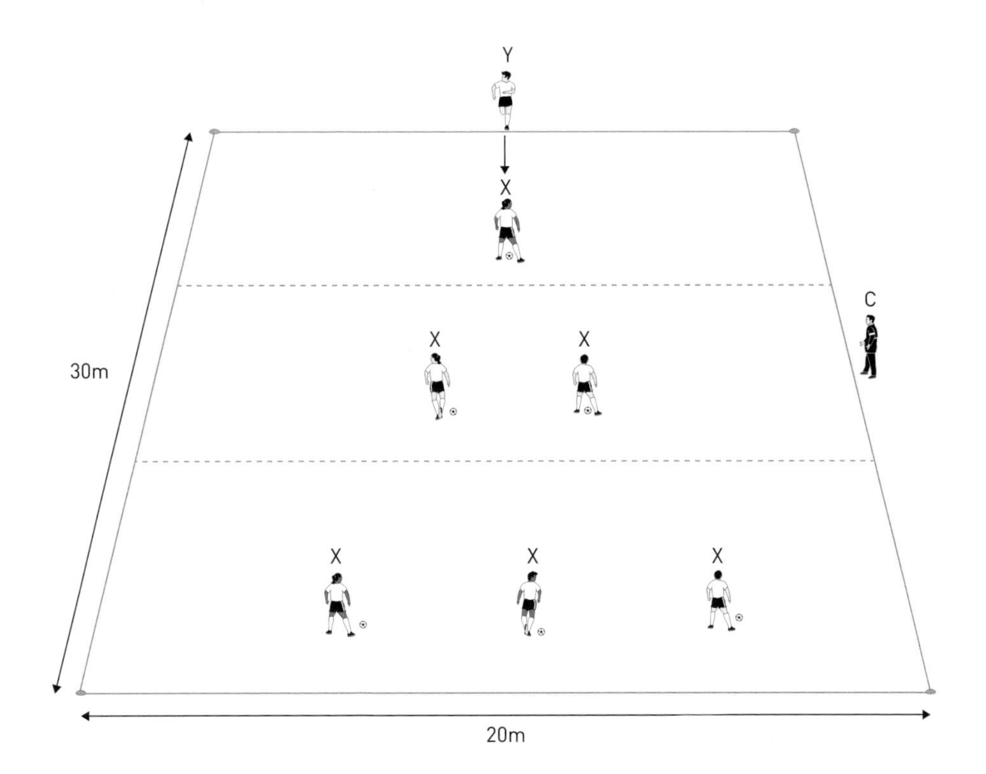

Organisation: Set out a 20 x 30m area and separate it into three smaller and equal-sized areas. Place one player in the first area, two players in the second area and three players in the final area. All of these players (X) have a ball which they dribble around their area. Set up a defender (Y) on the baseline of the area without a ball.

Equipment: Marker cones, footballs.

Description: The defender enters the first area and attempts to steal the ball from the first player. Once the ball is cleared from the area, the defender moves into the next area and attempts to clear the next two footballs. They continue until all footballs are cleared from all three of the areas. Rotate the defender and play again.

Key coaching points: Use your dribbling skills to keep the ball for as long as you can. Use your body to shield the ball from the defender. Use quick, and sharp turns to change direction to move away from the defender.

Progressions: Have a time limit per area, if the player manages to keep their ball in the area for the whole amount of time they win a point. Once a ball is cleared from the area with two or three players in, the tackled player (X) remains active and can help the other players (X) keep their footballs by passing to each other. When a player loses their ball, they then become the defender and move into the next area so that it becomes a continuous relay game.

››› 44 – 53 – 63 – 94

session 31 under the bridge

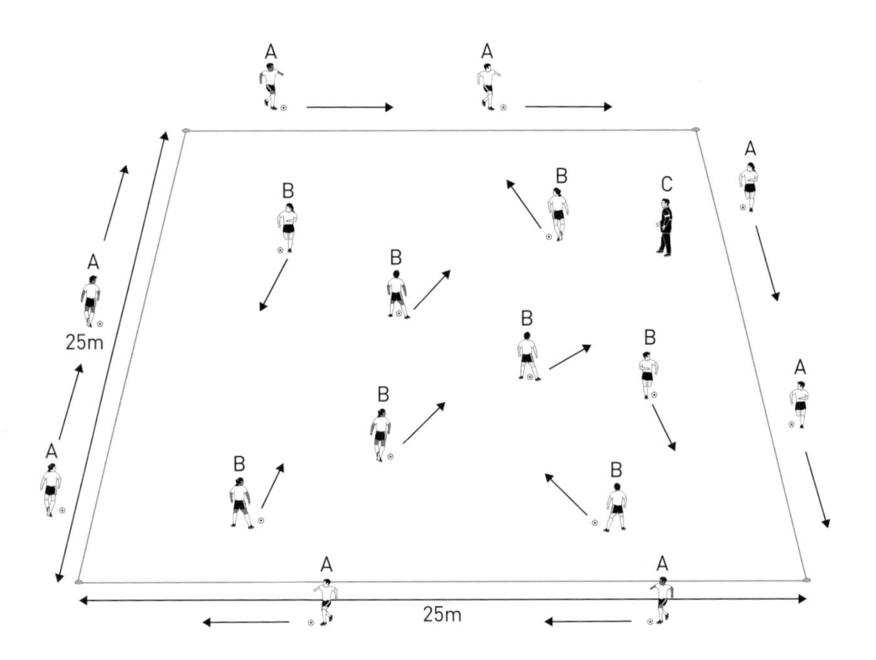

Organisation: Set out a 25 x 25m area. Organise players into two groups, A and B.

Equipment: Marker cones, footballs.

Description: Group A start with a ball each and dribble around the outside edges of the square in a clockwise direction. Group B start with a ball each and dribble around the inside of the square in any direction. When the coach calls 'Go', the players from group A dribble their footballs into the area and the players from group B pick their balls up, hold them above their heads and stand in a space with their legs apart. The players from Group A are then in a competition to see how many times they can play the ball through the legs (under the bridge) of a player from group B in one minute. Players can't play through the legs of the same player twice in a row. The teams then swap roles, and the player with the most points wins.

Key coaching points: Use your dribbling skills to keep the ball close to your feet. Use both feet to dribble the ball. Keep your head up, looking around for available bridges.

Progressions: Add some defenders to block the bridges. Dribble using your weaker foot only. Allow bridges to open and close as and when they choose.

››› 40 – 58 – 62 – 83

session 32 dribble, turn, pass, repeat

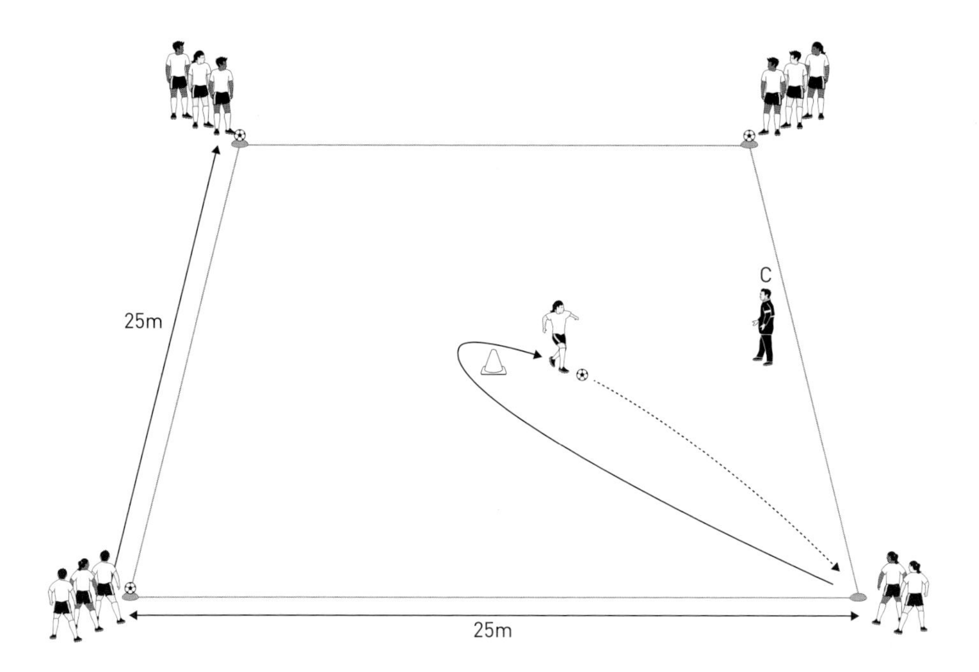

Organisation: Set out a 25 x 25m area with a football balanced on the cone at each corner. Organise players into four teams with one on each corner of the square. Place a traffic cone in the centre of the area and give the teams a ball each.

Equipment: Marker cones, traffic cones, footballs.

Description: When the coach calls 'Go', the first player on each team starts with the ball and dribbles out to and around the centre traffic cone. They then stop the ball and pass it aiming to knock the ball in their corner off the cone. If they knock it down, they score a point, reset and the next player goes. If they miss, the next player takes their turn. Play as a continuous relay with a time limit, whichever team score the most points wins.

Key coaching points: Use your dribbling skills to keep the ball close to your feet. Use both feet to dribble the ball. Use the inside of the foot for a more accurate pass.

Progressions: Dribble using your weaker foot only. Pass using your weaker foot only. Increase the size of the area to make the distance further for the dribble and the pass.

››› 34 – 49 – 61 – 98

session 33 the fabulous five

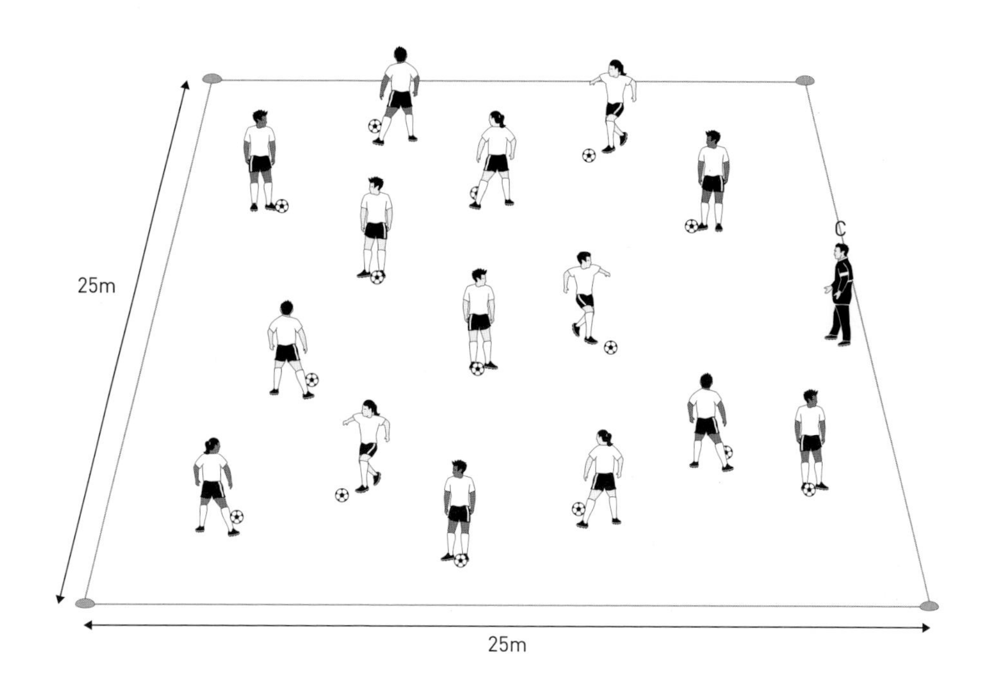

Organisation: Set out a 25 x 25m area. Give each player a ball and set them up in a space inside the area.

Equipment: Marker cones, footballs.

Description: The players dribble their football around the area listening for the Fabulous Five moves:

1 Toe Touch: Leave your ball where it is, toe touch three other footballs and return to your ball to carry on dribbling.

2 Knee Touch: Leave your ball where it is, knee touch three other footballs and return to your ball to carry on dribbling.

3 Nudge: Dribble your ball to another player and nudge them together, then carry on dribbling.

4 Sit: Leave your ball where it is, sit on three other footballs and return to your ball to carry on dribbling.

5 Swap: Swap your football with another player then carry on dribbling

Key coaching points: Use your dribbling skills to keep the ball close to your feet. Use both feet to dribble the ball. Listen and react quickly to the fabulous five commands.

Progressions: Extra bonus points to the players that complete the task the quickest. Take points away from players that don't have their ball under control or bump into other players. Dribble using your weaker foot only.

››› 35 - 36- 45 - 83

session 34 colour corridors

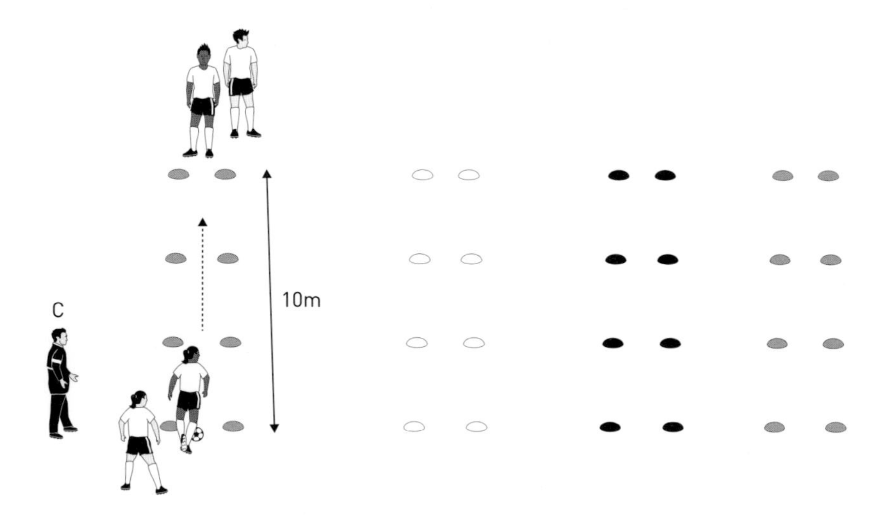

Organisation: Set out four corridors of different colour cones (red, yellow, etc.) about 10m in length with a gap of about 1m between each corridor. The first corridor is the widest with each corridor becoming progressively narrower.

Equipment: Marker cones, footballs.

Description: The players line up in equal numbers at each end of the first corridor and take it in turn to dribble the ball down the corridor using both feet before passing to their teammate at the other end and following their own pass in. The player that they pass to then does the same going back down the corridor and so on. If a player loses control of the ball while dribbling down the corridor, they are out. Once everyone has had a go at the first corridor, the players move on to the second that is narrower than the first and this then continues down the rest of the corridors until there is a winner.

Key coaching points: Keep the ball close to the feet when dribbling using both feet. Look up between touches. Try to use the correct weight and accuracy each time you pass, using the inside of the foot.

Progressions: Use a weaker foot to pass the ball. Try to do a skill as you dribble down each corridor before releasing the pass. Use smaller size balls to make them more difficult to control.

››› 32 – 56 – 57 – 84

session 35 figure of 8

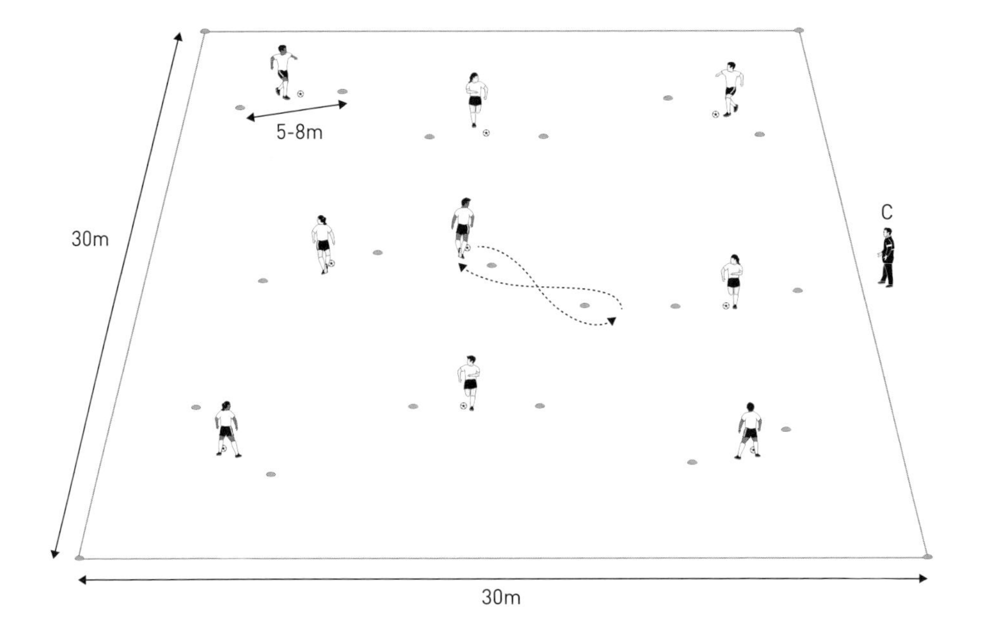

Organisation: Set out a 30 x 30m area. Give each player one ball and two cones, which they need to place on the floor 5–8m apart (depending on how much space you have).

Equipment: Marker cones, footballs.

Description: This is a technical practice where players work by themselves. The aim is to dribble the ball around the two cones in a figure of 8 practising five different ball familiarisation skills: 1 – right foot only; 2 – left foot only; 3 – inside of foot only; 4 – outside of foot only; 5- sole of foot only.

Key coaching points: Keep the ball close to the feet when dribbling. Take lots of small touches to keep the ball under control. Look up between touches.

Progressions: Use the cones as 'defenders' so the players can practise their turns. Use the cones as 'defenders' so the players can practise their skills and moves to beat a player. Pair players up to practise close control and ball skills against an actual defender.

››› 33 – 38 – 65 – 86

session 36 sing soccer

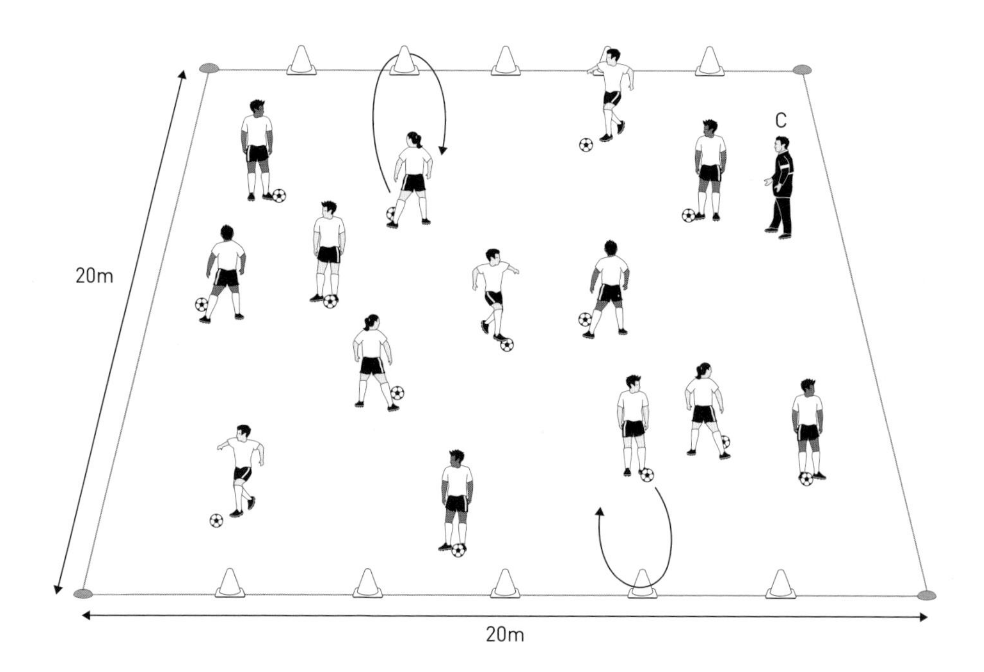

Organisation: Set out a 20 x 20m area with traffic cones placed on each baseline. Give the players a ball each.

Equipment: Marker cones, traffic cones, footballs.

Description: The coach whistles a tune or sings a song as the players dribble around the area. When the music stops, the players leave their footballs, run around the nearest cone and back to their own football as fast as possible.

Key coaching points: Keep the ball close to the feet when dribbling. Take lots of small touches to keep the ball under control. Look up and around between touches to see where the space is.

Progressions: Add a fun forfeit for the slowest player to return to their ball. Players have to return to a different ball. Players have to perform a turn or move to beat a player when they return to their football before they start dribbling again.

››› 45 – 43 – 64 – 86

session 37 turning circle

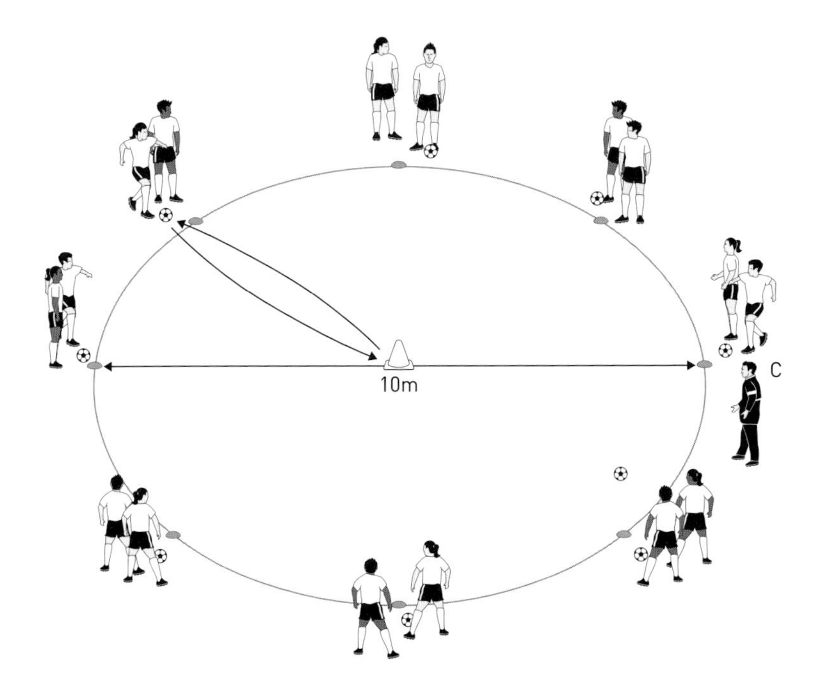

Organisation: Set out a circle using 8 marker cones. Place a traffic cone in the centre of the circle and organise the players into pairs, with a pair on each cone. Each pair needs a ball.

Equipment: Marker cones, traffic cone, footballs.

Description: The first player dribbles the ball out to the centre cone, performs a turn then dribbles the ball back to their partner for them to take their turn. Players must perform a different turn each time they dribble out to the centre cone.

Key coaching points: Keep the ball close to the feet when dribbling. Take lots of small touches to keep the ball under control. Turn sharply and quickly as if the traffic cone is a defender.

Progressions: Alternate turns using left foot and right foot only. Change to a pass back to partner after the player has performed the turn. After dribbling out to the middle, return the ball to the person to your right, creating a change of direction.

>>> 35 – 42 – 63 – 90

session 38 cone hunting

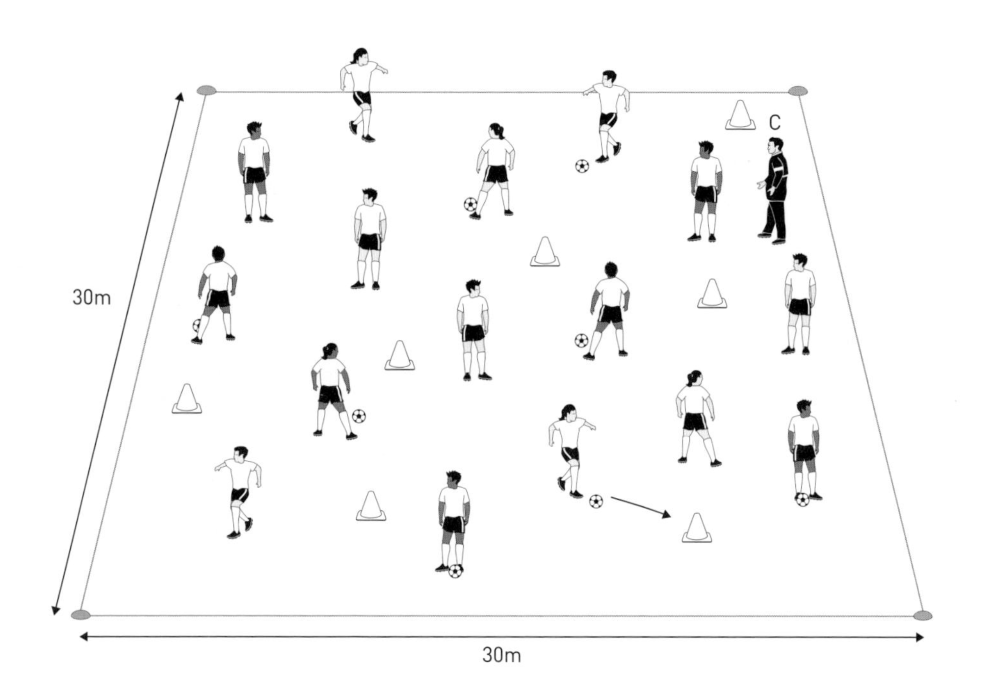

Organisation: Set out a 30 x 30m area with several traffic cones spread across the area.

Equipment: Marker cones, traffic cones, bibs, footballs.

Description: A number of traffic cones are distributed across the area. About half the players have footballs. They must try to win balls and then knock cones down. A player that succeeds must always set the cone up again before going after another ball. The player who knocks down the most cones wins.

Key coaching points: Close control dribbling. Vision of the entire playing area. 1 v 1 tactics. Speed of action.

Progressions: Introduce two defenders who become 'cone keepers' and try to prevent the cones from being knocked down. Divide the players and cones into two teams and set the cones out into two colours, one for each team, and state that each team can only knock down their specified colour.

››› 43 – 57 – 67 – 80

session 39 colour run

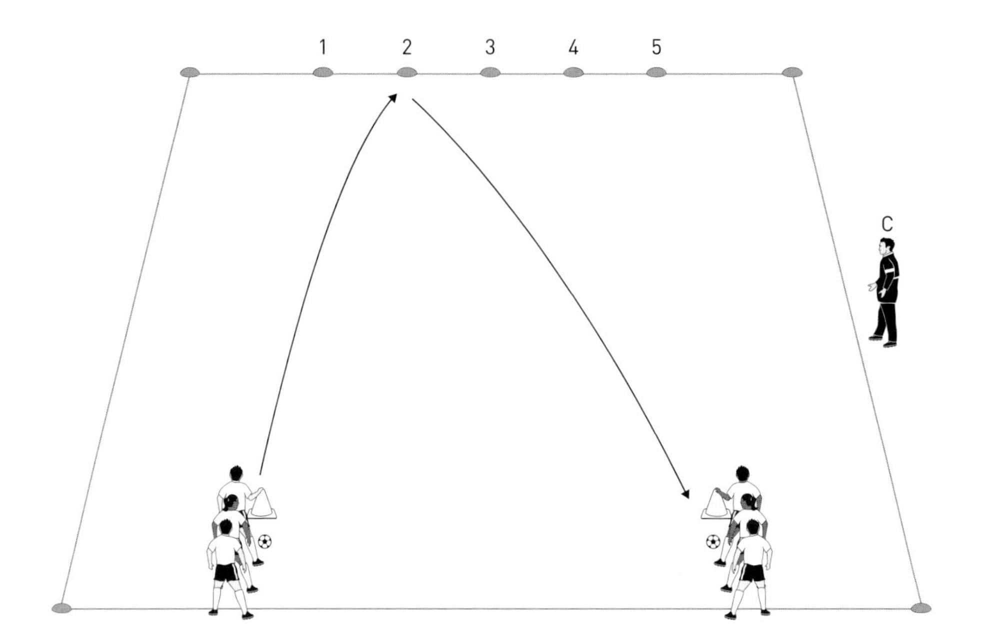

Organisation: Set out five small cones in a line and number them 1 to 5. Then mark out two traffic cones which are set at an equal distance away in line with the end numbered cones, to make a square. Organise players into two teams with a ball each, stationed behind one of the traffic cones.

Equipment: Marker cones, traffic cones, footballs.

Description: A player from each team stands with their hand on a corner traffic cone. When the coach calls a number, the two players dribble the football to touch the small cone with that number then back to their opponent's cone. The first player back in each pair scores a point and the first team to five points wins.

Key coaching points: Use both feet to dribble the ball. Push the ball a little further away from your feet so you can travel faster by running with the ball. Use quick and sharp turns to change direction to move away from the cones.

Progressions: Increase the distance between the numbered cones and the traffic cones. The coach calls more than one number or a set combination of numbers so they have to dribble to more than one marker cone in a go. Allow players to dribble only using their weaker foot.

››› 27 – 48 – 61 – 92

session 40 red square

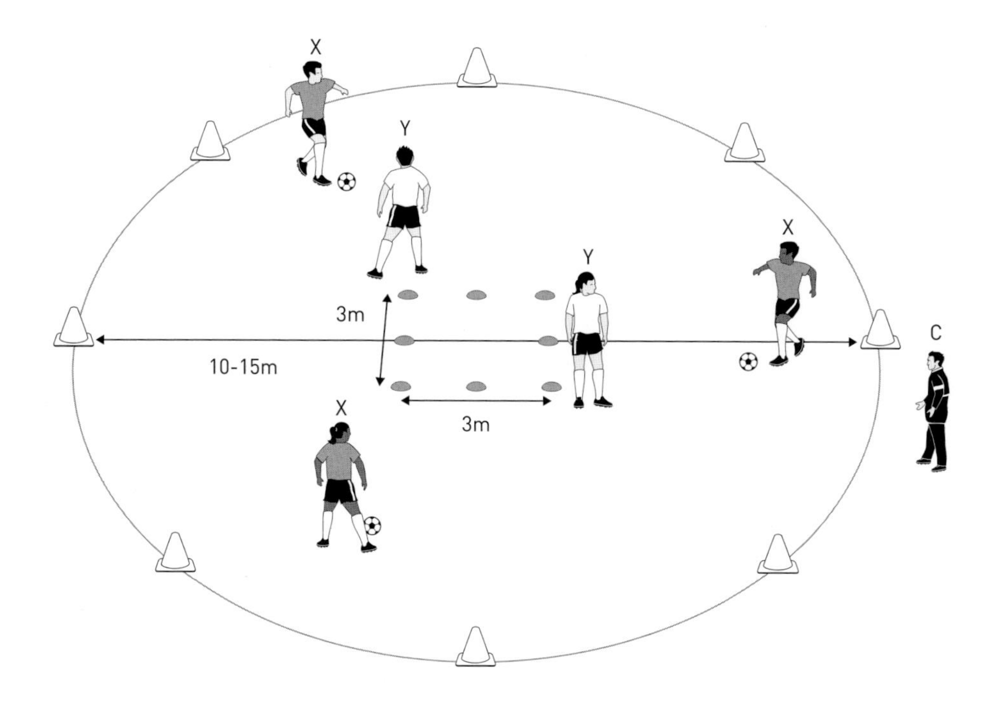

Organisation: Set out a 10–15m diameter circle with traffic cones and mark out a 3m square in the middle.

Equipment: Marker cones, traffic cones, footballs, bibs.

Description: Three attackers (X) start off in different parts of the circle against two defenders (Y) guarding the square in the middle. The aim of the game is for the attackers to dribble their ball into the centre square and stop it underfoot without the defenders tackling them. Once they have done this, they then go back into the circle to help out their teammates by offering themselves as passing opportunities so that they can move the ball into the circle and stop the ball underfoot. A point is awarded to the attackers for each ball they get into the square and a point is awarded to the defenders for each ball that they tackle off the attacker and then dribble out of the circle. The first team to 20 wins.

Key coaching points: Attacker – Keep the ball close to the feet when dribbling using both feet. Look up and around between touches. Use different skills to lose the defenders. Try to use the correct weight and accuracy each time you pass, using the inside of the foot when helping teammates to progress them into the square. Look for and create space.

Defender – Adopt the correct open body position for defending one-on-one and don't go to ground. Apply pressure and close players down especially when it is two-on-one or three-on-two attacking scenarios.

Progressions: Reduce the size of the circle or square. Introduce another attacker to make it more difficult for the defenders or more defenders to make it more difficult for the attackers.

››› 31 – 53 – 65 – 90

session 41 end to end

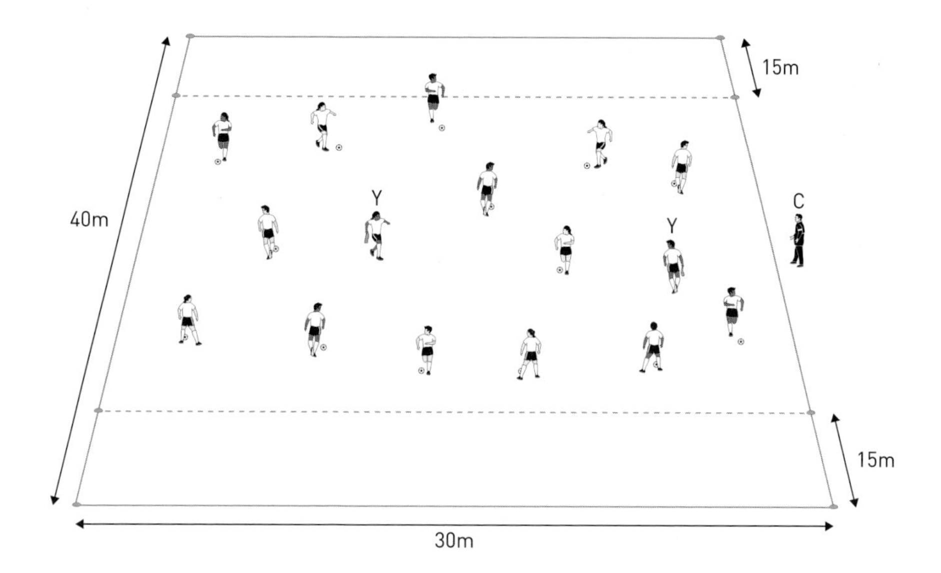

Organisation: Set out a 30 x 40m area, with two 15m zones at each end of the area. Each player has a ball, except for two defenders (Y) who hold a bib each.

Equipment: Cones, footballs, bibs.

Description: The players dribble their ball around the area aiming to avoid being tackled by the defenders (Y). If the defender wins the ball, they keep it and that attacker takes the bib and becomes the defender. When the coach calls 'Go', all players leave their footballs and bibs and race to the zones at each end. The two players that are slowest to react and make it across to one of the zones become the first two defenders for the next round.

Key coaching points: Keep the ball close to the feet when dribbling using both feet. Look up and around between touches. Use different skills and turns to keep your ball away from the defenders. Use your body to shield the ball and keep it under your control.

Progressions: Increase the number of defenders per round. On 'Go', the players travel to the other zone with their ball, dribbling across. Decrease the size of the zones, therefore restricting space to dribble.

››› 24 – 57 – 64 – 97

session 42 football pinball

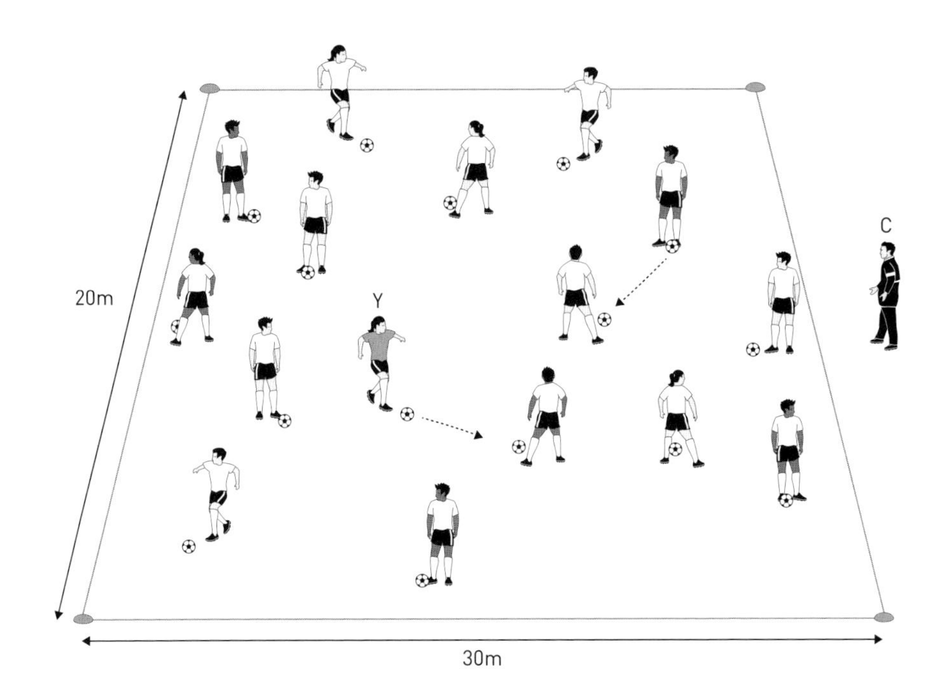

Organisation: Set out a 30 x 20m area. Give each player a football and select two 'catchers' (Y).

Equipment: Marker cones, bibs, footballs.

Description: The players dribble their footballs around the area attempting to avoid the 'catchers' (Y). The catchers aim to eliminate the other players by passing their football so that it hits the other players' balls.

Key coaching points: Keep the ball close to the feet when dribbling using both feet. Look up and around between touches for the catchers. Use different skills and turns to keep your ball away from the catchers.

Progressions: Players are only eliminated if the ball that gets hit leaves the area. Catchers can only pass the ball using their weaker foot. Add a time limit.

››› 37 – 60 – 63 – 75

session 43 shark tank

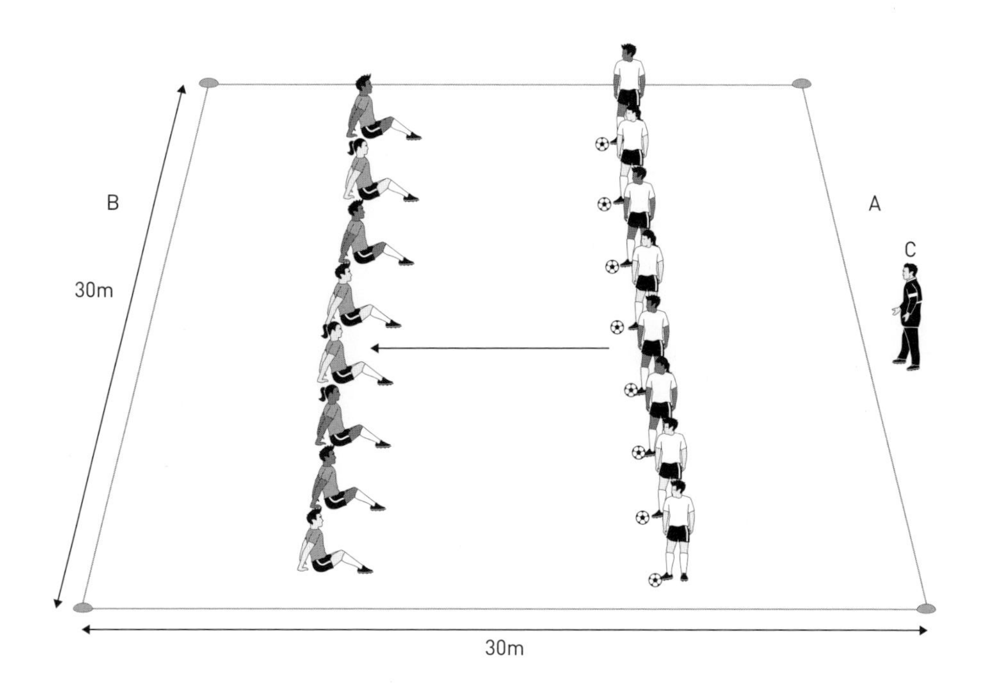

Organisation: Set out a 30 x 30m area. Divide the players into two groups.

Equipment: Marker cones, bibs, footballs.

Description: Half of the players ('sharks') sit on the ground without balls. The other players have a ball each. The players try to dribble past the sharks from one end line (A) to the other (B). The sharks try to steal the balls as they pass. Each crossing scores one point. If a player loses their ball to a shark, the two players immediately switch roles. Who can score the most points?

Key coaching points: Close control dribbling. Vision of the entire playing area. 1 v 1 tactics. Speed of action.

Progression: Increase the number of sharks. Allow sharks to be standing.

››› 38 – 53 – 68 – 96

session 44 goal-den gates

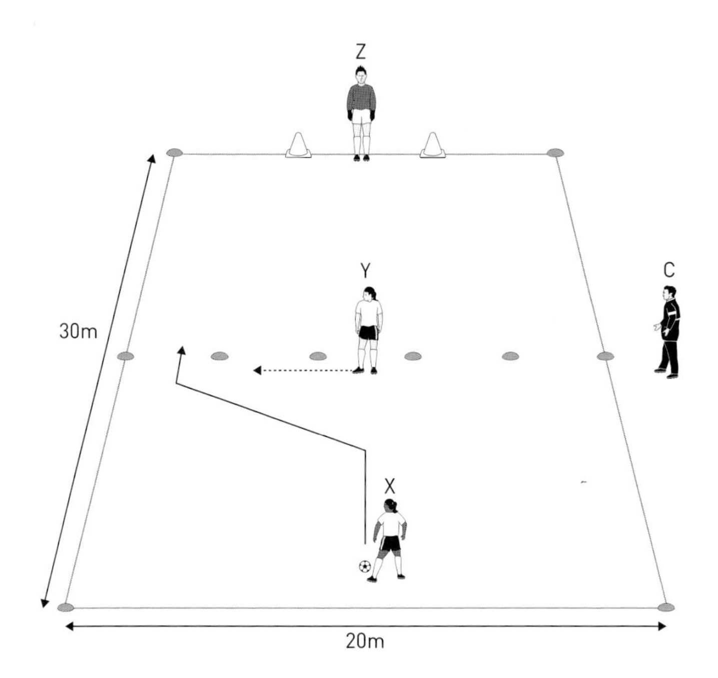

Organisation: Set out a 20 x 30m area, with a goal at one end and three small gates across the middle of the area. One player is a goalkeeper (Z). Organise the rest of the players into pairs – one attacker (X) and one defender (Y).

Equipment: Marker cones, traffic cones, football.

Description: The attacking player starts with the ball and dibbles towards the goal, aiming to travel through a gate and then score a goal. The defender attempts to stop the attacker from scoring by stealing the ball as they go through a gate and dribbling it back over the baseline. Once the attack is over, change the players' roles and repeat. The first player to score three goals wins.

Key coaching points: Use both feet to dribble the ball. Shoot using your laces or instep for power, or inside of the foot for accuracy. Use tricks and skills to beat the defender.

Progressions: Reduce the number of gates to limit the attacker's options. Limit the attacker to two touches once they have passed through the gate, encouraging a quick shot at goal. Develop into a 2 v 2 or a 3 v 3.

››› 30 – 49 – 67 – 100

session 45 knights & dragons

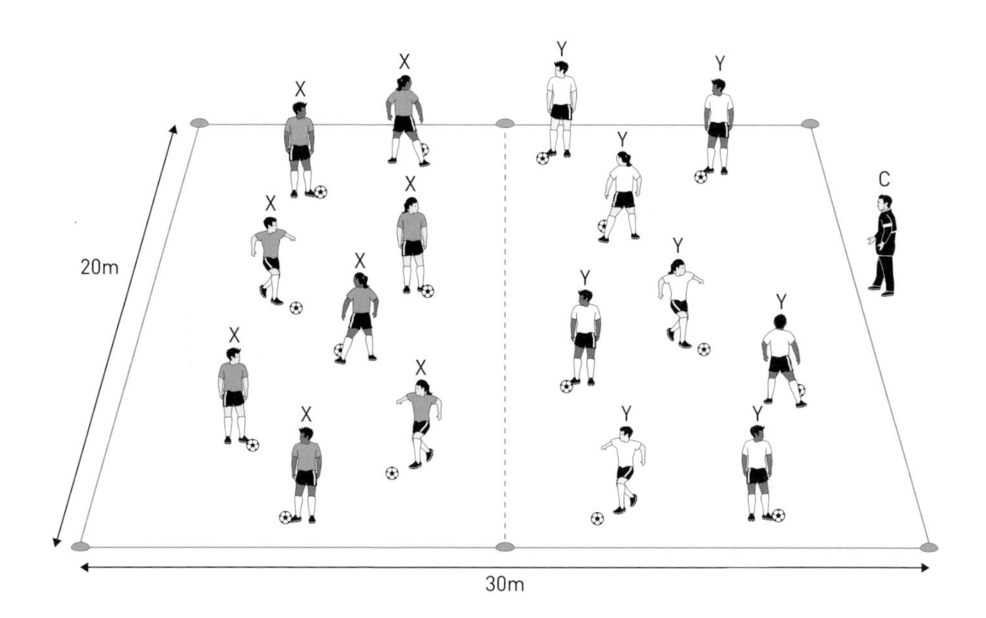

Organisation: Set out a 30 x 20m area with a dividing line going across lengthways, dividing the area into two equal halves. Players are divided into two teams – knights (X) and dragons (Y) – with a team in each half of the area. Players have a football each and are allocated a specific opponent on the opposite team.

Equipment: Marker cones, bibs, footballs.

Description: The players dribble their footballs around their half of the area. When the coach calls out 'knights' or 'dragons', the players in that team dribble across into their opponents' half and attempt to catch their partner by tagging them as they dribble. When all the opposition are tagged the game is over, and each team returns to their half and the game begins again.

Key coaching points: Keep the ball close to the feet when dribbling using both feet. Look up and around between touches. Use different skills and turns to keep your ball away from the defenders. Use your body to shield the ball and keep it under your control.

Progressions: Allow players to use the whole of the area once the coach has called out 'knights' or 'dragons'. Players attempt to catch their partner by kicking their ball out of the area.

››› 36 – 40 – 61 – 90

session 46 weighted passes

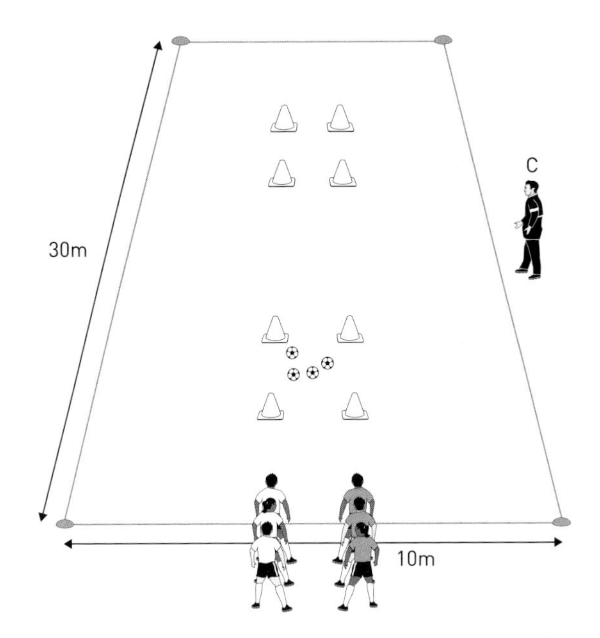

Organisation: Set out a 10 x 30m area. With traffic cones, mark out a small square near the baseline and another small square at the other side of the area, 15–20m away. The square nearer the baseline has four balls in it. Organise players into teams of three or four at the baseline of the area. Repeat for the correct number of players.

Equipment: Marker cones, traffic cones, footballs.

Description: One at a time, the players run to collect a ball from the first square and attempt to pass the ball so that it stops inside the second square. If the player misses the ball, it is collected and placed back in the first square and the next player in that team takes their turn. The first team to successfully pass their four footballs into the end square wins.

Key coaching points: Pass using inside of the foot. Correct placement of standing foot. Correct weight of pass.

Progressions: Add more footballs into the square. Increase the distance between the two squares. Pass using left or right foot only.

››› 49 – 59 – 61 – 101

session 47 pass point

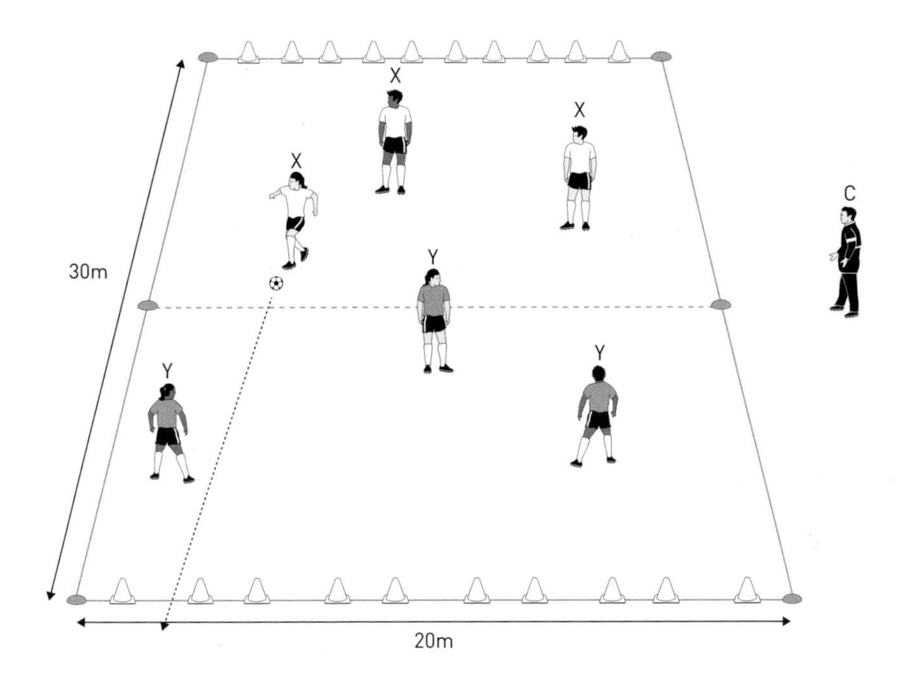

Organisation: Set out a 20 x 30m area with a central line dividing the area into two halves. Place traffic cones along each of the baselines creating five small goals, which are each given a points value. Organise players into two teams and position one team in each half of the area as a 3 v 3.

Equipment: Marker cones, traffic cones, bibs, footballs.

Description: Each team aims to score points by passing the ball along the floor so that it passes through one of the small goals on the opponent's base line. For every successful pass, the team score the amount of points allocated to that goal. All players must stay in their own half and may try to stop the ball going into the small goals by using only their feet. The first team to reach 20 points wins.

Key coaching points: Pass to your teammates to create space for an attempt at goal. Use the inside of the foot to pass. Go for goal as soon as an opportunity arises.

Progressions: Only score using weaker foot. Only score with a first-time pass. Allow one defender into the opposition half to apply pressure to the ball.

››› 49 – 51 – 68 – 82

session 48 two-touch tennis

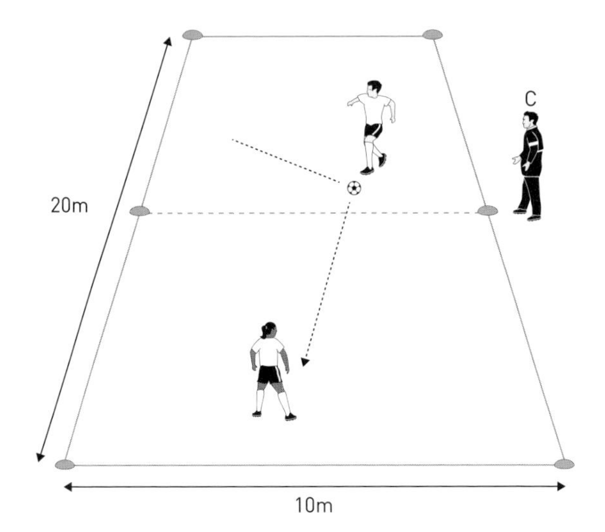

Organisation: Mark out a 10 x 20m area with a dividing line across the middle of the area. One player stands in each half of the area. Repeat the area for the total number of players.

Equipment: Marker cones, bibs, football.

Description: Playing 1 v 1 and positioned inside their own half, each player is only allowed two touches to return the ball into their opponent's half of the area. If a player makes a mistake or is unable to return the pass with two touches, their opponent wins one point. First to eleven points wins.

Key coaching points: Pass using inside of the foot. Correct weight of pass. Be alert and ready for the return.

Progressions: Pass using weaker foot only. Only take one touch with each foot. Increase or decrease the size of the area depending on level of development.

››› 28 – 60 – 70 – 84

session 49 target pass

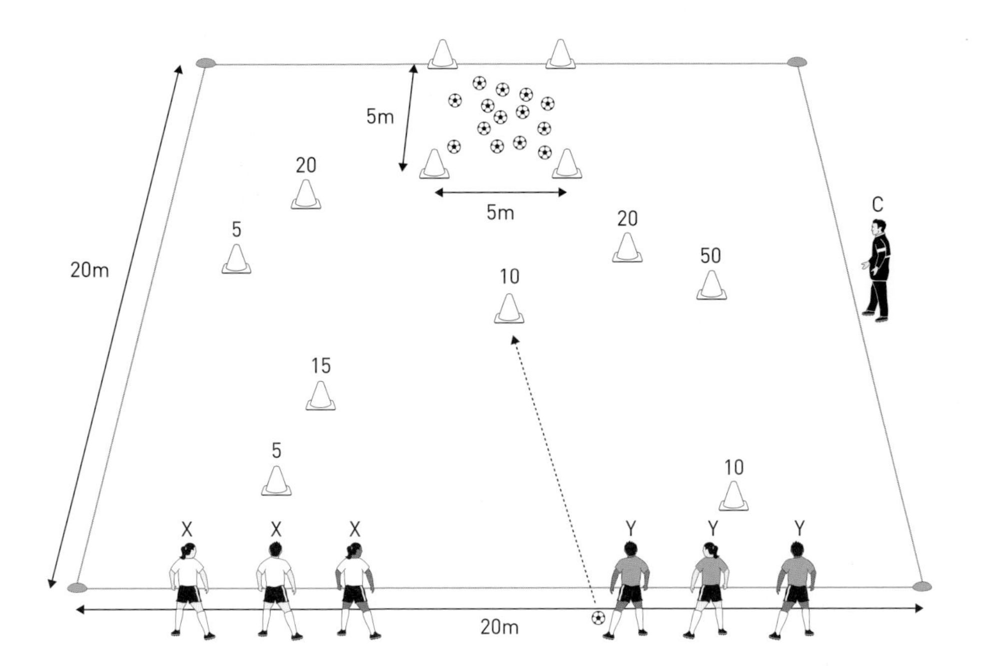

Organisation: Set out a 20 x 20m area with a number of traffic cones scattered randomly around the area. Label each cone with a points value – 5, 10, 15, 20 and 50. Create a 5 x 5m 'ball pit' at one end of the area and fill it with footballs. Organise players into two teams of three (X and Y).

Equipment: Marker cones, traffic cones, bibs, footballs.

Description: When the coach shouts 'Go', the first player on each team races around the outside of the area to collect a ball from the 'ball pit', then back to the start point. The player then attempts to pass the ball and knock down one of the traffic cones to score points. Whichever cone the ball knocks over, the team scores that amount of points and if the pass is unsuccessful, the ball must be replaced into the ball pit. The first team to score 100 points wins!

Key coaching points: Pass using inside of the foot. Correct weight of pass. Keep the ball close to your feet when dribbling back to start point.

Progressions: Dribble and pass only using weaker foot. Increase or decrease the amount of target cones. Add a defender into the area who is allowed to block passes.

››› 37 – 44 – 46 – 85

session 50 chips

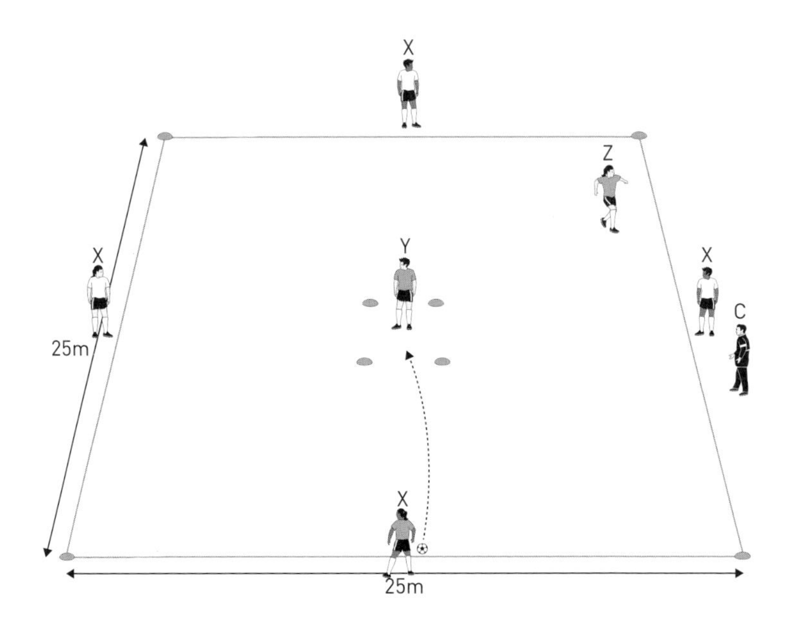

Organisation: Set out a 25 x 25m area with a small square in the middle. Organise a team of four players (X) with one on each side of the area, one player (Y) standing inside the central square and a defender (Z) who can move around inside the square but is not allowed inside the small central square

Equipment: Marker cones, bibs, football.

Description: The players on the outside (X) pass the ball around the edges of the area. They score a point by attempting to chip the ball to player Y in the central square so that they catch the ball. The defender attempts to stop the chipped pass by blocking with their feet or head, but not their hands. If the pass is blocked, the player (X) that attempted the chip becomes the defender (Z), and if it is successful, they swap with player Y in the central square.

Key coaching points: Strike the bottom of the ball in order to get it off the ground. Pass the ball around the edge to make space for a clear chip to the centre player. Aim to only take two touches, one to receive and one to pass.

Progressions: Only chip the ball to the centre player with a first-touch attempt. Add an extra defender. May only chip the ball using weaker foot.

››› 46 – 55 – 66 – 78

session 51 bounce ball

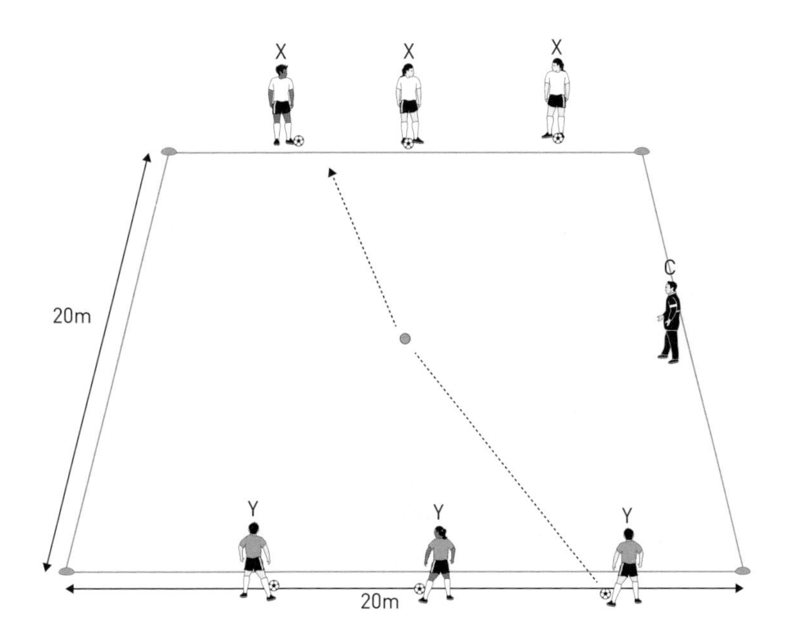

Organisation: Set out a 20 x 20m area with one ball placed in the centre of the area. This ball needs to be a different size or colour to the other football used during the game – i.e. a dodgeball. This game works best in an indoor sports hall or school hall. Organise players into two teams (X and Y) and set up the players on opposite baselines with a football each.

Equipment: Marker cones, bibs, footballs, different colour/size ball.

Description: Arrange the players behind each baseline of the area and give out three footballs per team. Players must stay behind their baseline and pass their footballs in order to try to hit the centre ball and bounce it forward towards the other team's baseline. The first team to bounce the centre ball past the other team's baseline wins the game.

Key coaching points: Pass the footballs using the inside of the foot. Use the correct weight of pass when aiming for the centre ball. Use the correct placement of standing foot.

Progressions: Make the centre ball smaller (tennis ball) to make the target harder to hit so passes need to be more accurate. Players have to make one pass to a teammate along their own baseline before they can make an attempt at the centre ball. Increase the distance of the baselines to make the pass from further away.

>>> 56 – 60 – 69 – 77

session 52 dodge it

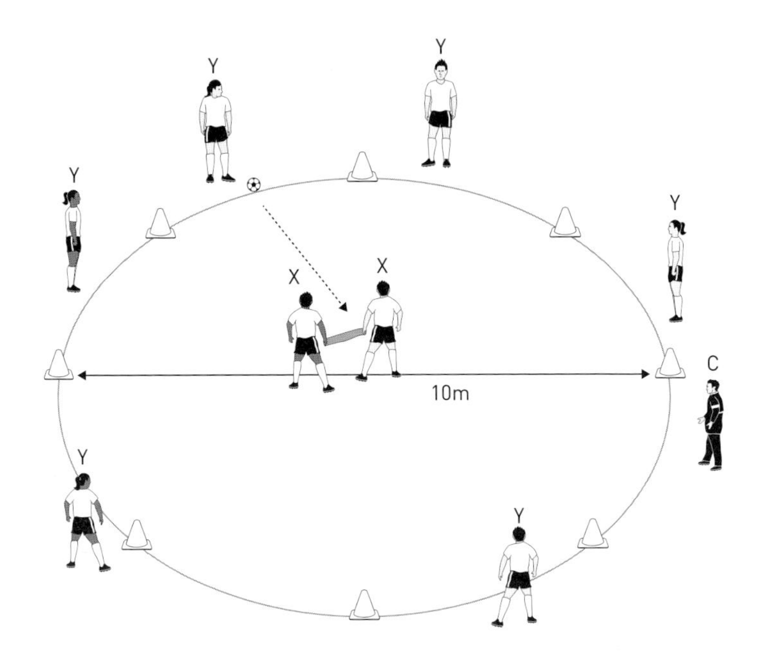

Organisation: Set out a circle 10 metres in diameter with marker cones. Position six players (Y) on the outside of the circle and two players (X) on the inside, holding one end of a bib between them so they are joined as a pair.

Equipment: Traffic cones, bib, football.

Description: The players (Y) around the edge of the circle pass the football aiming to hit either of the two players (X) in the middle below the waist. Each time a player in the middle is hit that pair gains one point. Swap turns after 30 seconds and once all players have had a turn in the middle, the pair with the lowest score is the winner!

Key coaching points: Pass using inside of the foot. Correct weight of pass.

Progressions: Make the circle bigger or smaller. Only allow Y players outside of the circle to pass using their weaker foot. Add a second ball.

››› 26 – 56 – 62 – 81

session 53 3 v 1 to 1 v 1

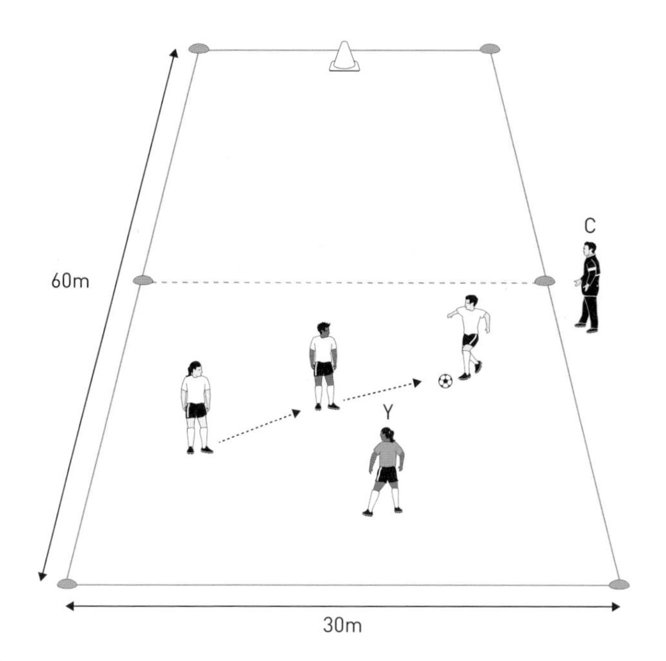

Organisation: Set out a 60 x 10m area and divide it in half down the middle. Place one traffic cone at the end of one of the halves. Set up four players in the opposite half to the cone, one of which will be the defender (Y).

Equipment: Marker cones, bibs, traffic cones, football.

Description: Play 3 v 1 inside the empty half of the area. The objective is for the three X players to make five successful passes as a team against the defender. Once the three players make five passes, one of them may enter one half with the ball and attempt to score a point by knocking the cone down. The defender may also enter the other half to defend the cone and wins a point if they successfully defend the attack.

Key coaching points: Move to create space to pass during the 3 v 1. Accurate pass to knock down the cone to score a point. Use your skills to beat the defender during the 1 v 1.

Progressions: Make the cone into a small goal or gate. Increase the number of passes needed before they can attempt to score a point. Add a second defender to create a 3 v 2.

>>> **41 – 48 – 61 – 75**

session 54 speedy strikers

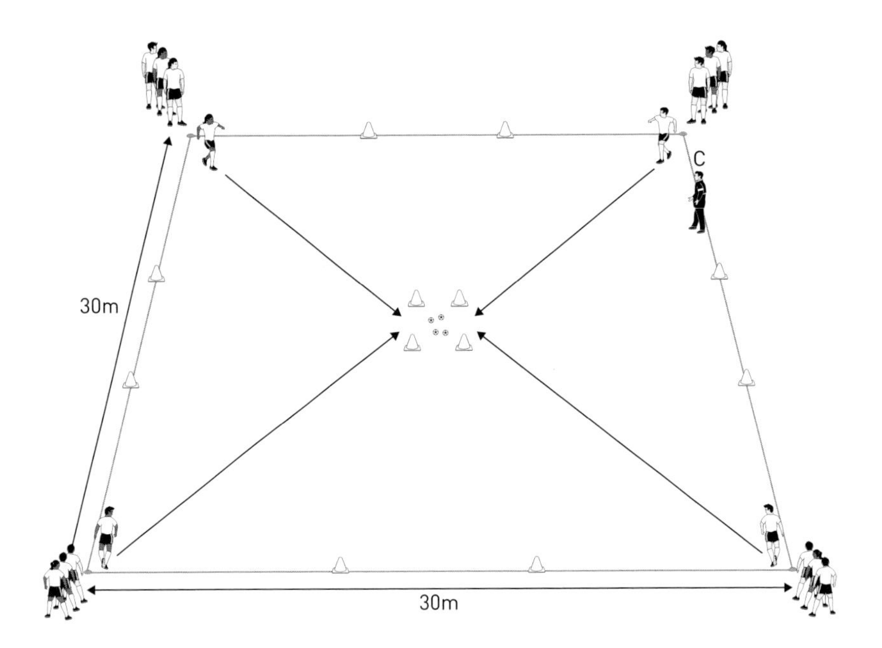

Organisation: Set out a 30 x 30m area with four goals, one on each line, marked with traffic cones and a small square in the centre. Set players up into four teams and place four footballs in the centre square.

Equipment: Marker cones, traffic cones, footballs.

Description: When the coach calls 'Go', the first player from each team races out to collect a ball from the centre square and attempts to score in one of the four goals. Only one player can attack each of the goals at any time, so they need to find a goal each. If the player misses, they do not score any points, and if they score a goal, they get one point for their team. If they are the first player to score for that round, they get an additional bonus point.

Key coaching points: React quickly to get to the ball and attack one of the goals. Shoot using your laces (on the top of the boot) for power and your instep for accuracy.

Progressions: After taking the ball from the centre square, only take one more touch for the shot at goal. Add a defender to create a 1 v 1. Shoot using your weaker foot only.

››› 32 – 53 – 63 – 100

session 55 the cube

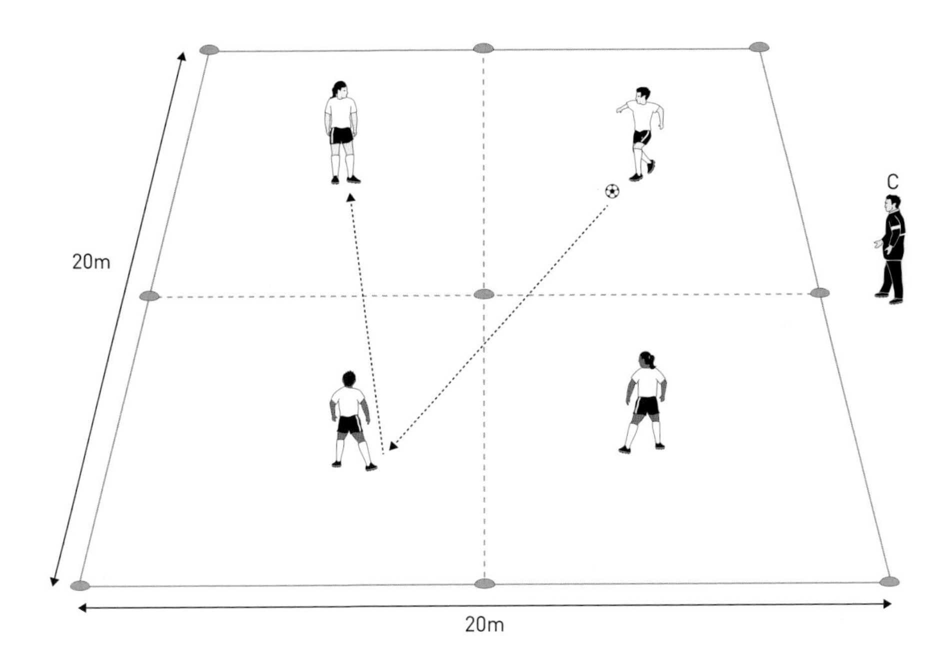

Organisation: Set out a 20 x 20m area and divide it into four equal sections. Place one player in each section of the square.

Equipment: Marker cones, football.

Description: One player starts with the ball in their square and passes it to a player in any of the other squares. The receiving player must then take a maximum of two touches to return it into another player's square. If the player is unable to return the ball into another square, the other three players score a point. The pass must be made to feet and not just smashed aimlessly across the square but can be made in any direction. The first player to 10 points wins.

Key coaching points: Pass using inside of the foot. Correct weight of pass. Be alive and alert in order to react to the direction of each pass.

Progressions: Only use one foot to control, then the other to pass. Only use weaker foot for both touches. Add an extra player on the outside of the area, when one player makes an error they swap with the player on the outside.

››› 48 – 56 –70 – 95

session 56 minefield

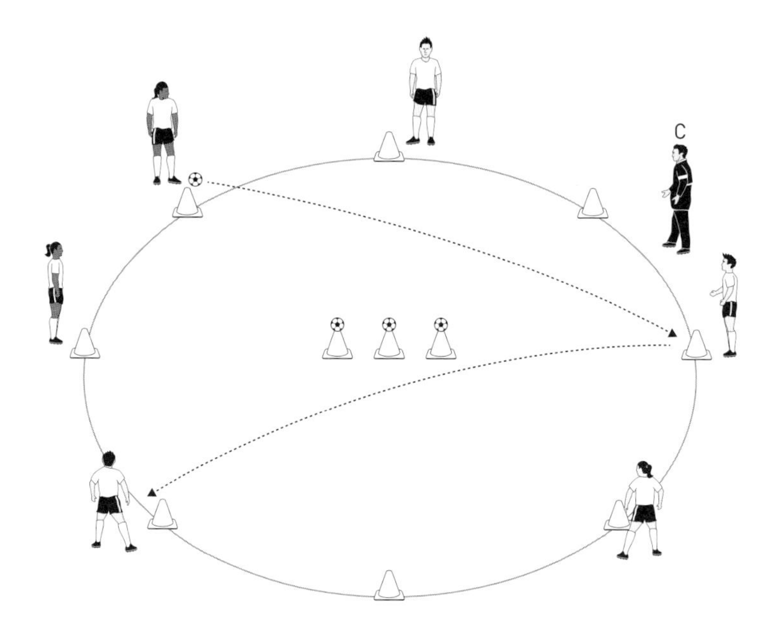

Organisation: Set out a circle using eight traffic cones. Station six players on the perimeter of the circle standing behind the cones, leaving two empty spaces. Balance three balls on top of cones in the centre of the circle.

Equipment: Traffic cones, footballs.

Description: The six players work as a team to pass the ball across the circle without detonating the mines (knocking down any of the three footballs). Once the player has made a pass, they move into one of the two empty spaces behind the cones, creating movement and new angles for passes across the circle.

Key coaching points: Pass using inside of the foot. Accuracy of passes. Be on your toes and ready to receive a pass.

Progressions: Only use one foot to control, then the other to pass. Only use weaker foot for both touches. Once a player detonates a mine they are eliminated, leaving less players and more spaces. The final player left wins.

››› 55 – 47 – 63 – 73

session 57 magic ball

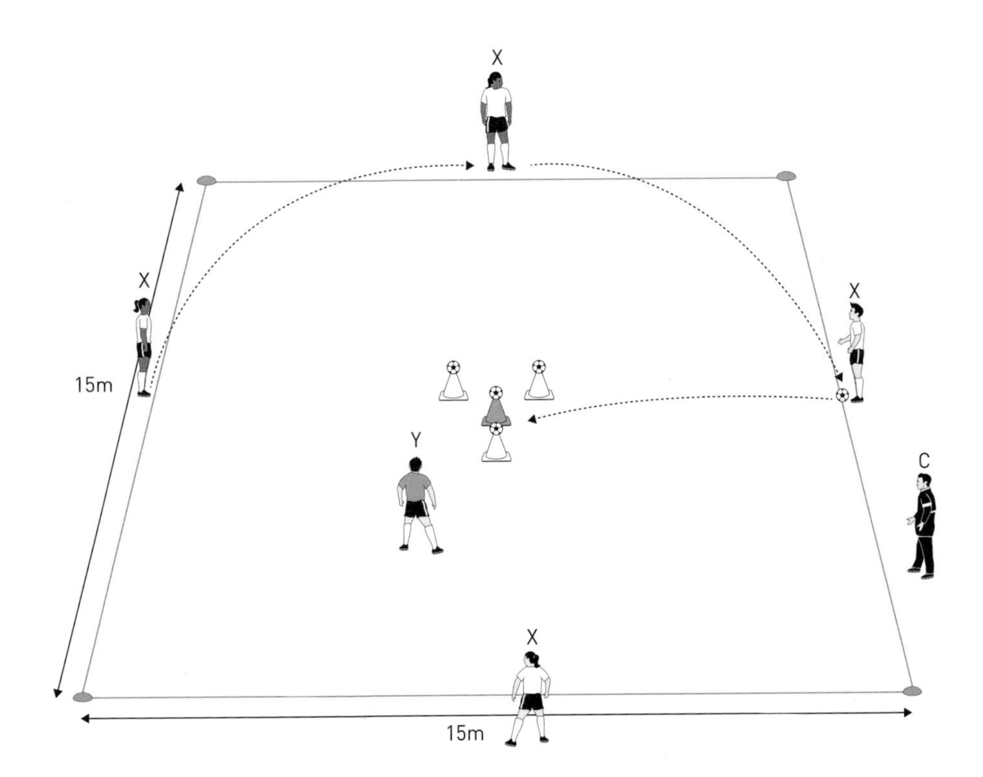

Organisation: Set out a 15 x 15m area, set out in a triangle in the centre of the area with three footballs balanced on a cone each. Set up one extra ball balanced on a cone in the middle of the triangle. This is the 'magic' ball. Organise players into groups of five, with four players (X) positioned on each side of the square and one player (Y) in the middle area who acts as the defender.

Equipment: Marker cones, traffic cones, bibs, footballs.

Description: The X players pass the ball to each other around the outside of the area and work as a team to create enough space to take a shot at the central footballs without the defender (Y) being able to block the shot. If they manage to knock down one of the footballs, the defender (Y) gets one point, and if they knock down the central 'magic' ball, the defender gets three points. All footballs need to be placed back on the cone each time they are knocked off. Play for three minutes then rotate the defender. The player that gets the fewest points during their turn is the winner.

Key coaching points: Pass using inside of the foot. Correct weight of pass. Move the ball quickly away from the defender to create the space for an effort at the central footballs and the 'magic' ball.

Progressions: Add a second defender to work as a pair. Players have to knock down all three footballs before they are allowed to aim for the 'magic' ball; this time once the ball is knocked down it stays off. Players have to knock down all three footballs before they are allowed to aim for the 'magic' ball, but if they knock down the 'Magic' ball before knocking down the other three footballs, all balls are replaced and they have to start again.

››› 42 – 60 – 68 – 87

session 58 tunnel vision

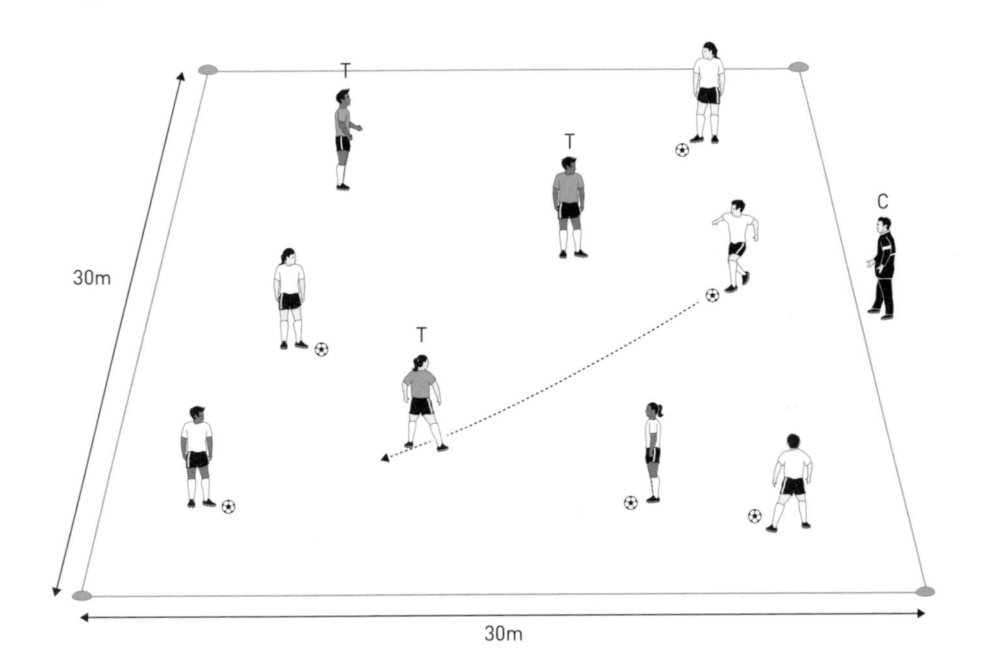

Organisation: Set out a 30 x 30m area. Divide players into a team of six and a team of three. Players in the team of six have a football each.

Equipment: Marker cones, bibs, footballs.

Description: Play 6 v 3 in the area. Three numbered 'tunnel players' (T) wear a bib and move around the area. At the coach's signal, the first tunnel player stops and creates a 'tunnel' between their legs. When they stop, the other players immediately try and pass a ball through the tunnel. After three successful tunnel shots, the player closes the tunnel, the coach whistles again, and the second player becomes the tunnel. After three more shots, it is the third player's turn, before starting again with the first player. Who can score the most tunnel shots?

Key coaching points: Looking up from the ball. Close ball control. Speed of action. Passing with the inside of the foot.

Progressions: Divide the players into groups of three and number the players 1, 2 or 3. The game starts with players 2 and 3 playing 1 v 1 scoring by passing through player 1's 'tunnel' goal. When the coaches signal, the tunnels are rotated. The player with the most points in their group wins.

››› 31 – 56 – 62 – 71

session 59 happy hoops

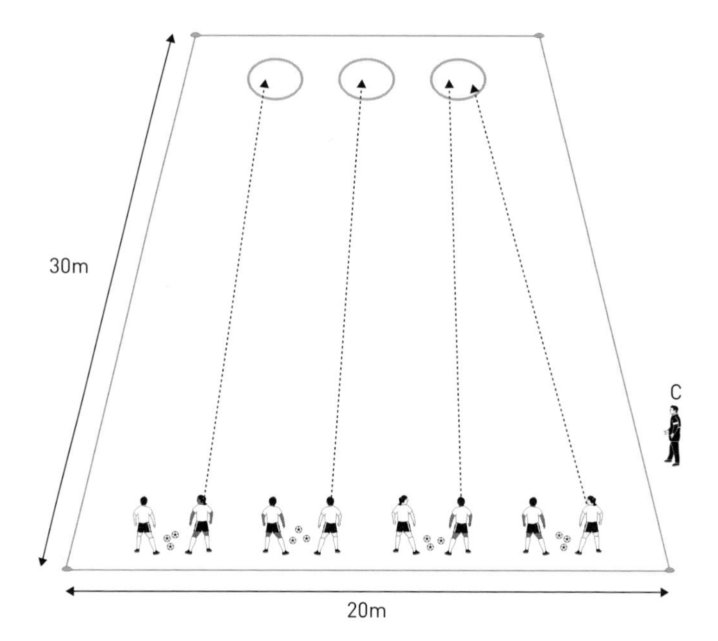

Organisation: Set out a 20 x 30m area and place three hoops along one end. Divide players into four pairs and give each pair three footballs, then position the players along the baseline of the area.

Equipment: Marker cones, footballs, hoops.

Description: Each team attempts to pass their footballs into the hoops at the opposite end. Each team may only pass one ball at a time and teams must alternate turns. If their pass is unsuccessful, they must retrieve their ball and their partner has the next attempt. Once a successful pass stays in the hoop, they must aim for a different hoop until they have passed their three footballs into the three different hoops. The first team with three balls in three hoops wins.

Key coaching points: Pass using inside of the foot. Correct weight of pass. Dribble the ball back to your partner after an unsuccessful pass.

Progressions: Pass using left or right foot only. Increase or stagger the distance of the three hoops. Increase the number of hoops.

››› 46 – 54 – 66 – 94

session 60 2 v 1 passing target

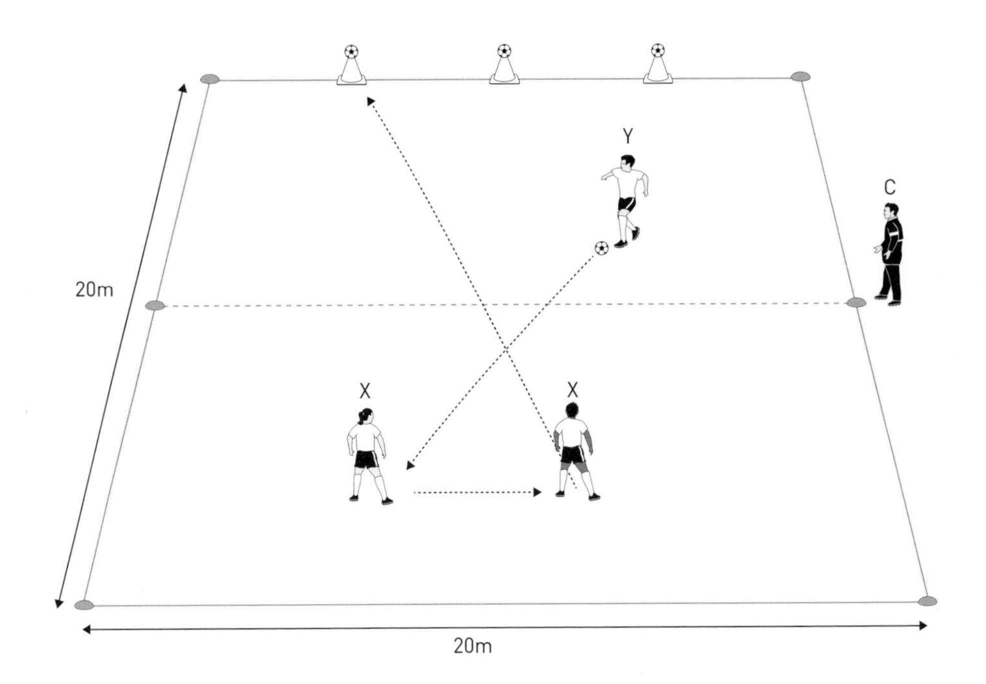

Organisation: Set out a 20 x 20m area and balance three footballs on top of traffic cones at one end. Mark out a halfway line across the area. Divide the players into groups of three with two players (X) in one half with a ball and one player (Y) in the other half defending the three footballs on the cones.

Equipment: Marker cones, traffic cones bibs, balls.

Description: The defender (Y) starts with the ball and passes it to one of the players in the opposite half. The two attacking players (X) pass to each other in an attempt to open up some space for a shot at one of the three footballs. The defender may move from side to side to defend the three balls from the shot, but must stay inside their own half of the area. If the attackers successfully knock a ball down, they gain a point. Rotate the defender after each attempt.

Key coaching points: Pass using inside of the foot. Correct weight of pass. Pass the ball quickly to open us space for a shot.

Progressions: Pass using left or right foot only. Add an extra defender to create a 2 v 2. Remove the halfway line to create a small-sided practice.

››› 32 – 57 – 64 – 99

session 61 speed demons

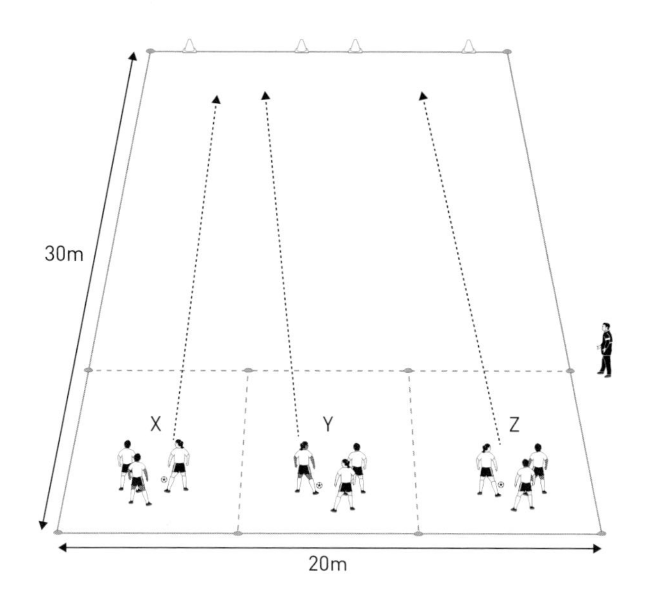

Organisation: Set out a 20 x 30m area, with two small goals set up on either side of the base line. Organise players into three teams of three (X, Y and Z), and set them up in three smaller areas at the opposite end of the playing area, with one ball per team.

Equipment: Marker cones, footballs, bibs.

Description: The players in each team pass the ball between themselves using only two touches. As the coach calls 'Go', the player with the ball turns out of their small square and races to either of the goals attempting to score before the players from the other two teams. The first two players to score win a point for their team. If the shot misses or the player is the slowest, no points are awarded. First team to score 10 goals wins!

Key coaching points: Accurate passes in your small teams using inside of the foot. Use your pace and dribbling skills to get to the goals quickly. Accurate shots at goal to score a point.

Progressions: Limit the number of touches the players can take before they are allowed to shoot at goal. Whichever player is in possession when the coach calls 'Go' makes a through ball pass into space for a teammate to run onto. Add a goalkeeper to each goal.

››› 25 – 34 – 53 – 77

session 62 first-time finish

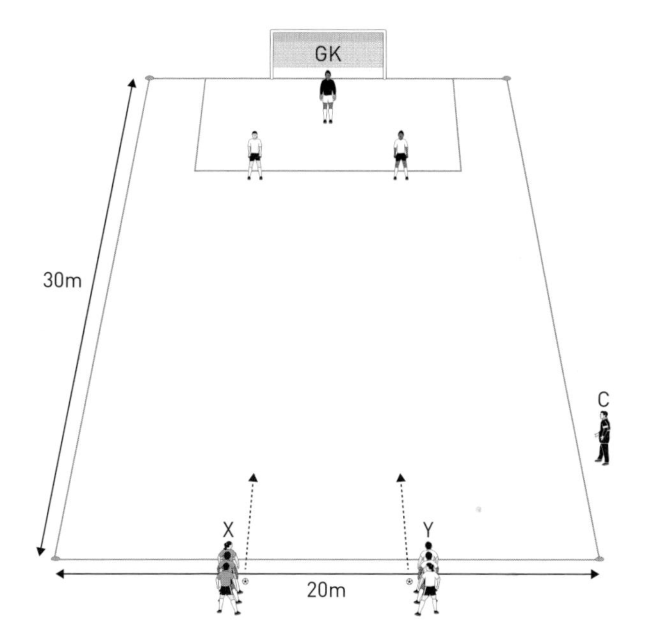

Organisation: Set out a 20 x 30m area with a goal at one end. Split players into two teams of four, with an additional goalkeeper (GK) in the goal on the edges of the penalty area.

Equipment: Goal, marker cones, bibs, footballs.

Description: The first player stands on the edge of the penalty area facing their team, with their back to goal. The second player in the line passes the ball through the first player's legs so that they can turn, run onto the ball and shoot first time. The second player then moves to the edge of the penalty area ready to be set up for their shot at goal and the players continue to rotate. The two teams take alternate shots, and 10 goals wins.

Key coaching points: Correct weight of pass to set up shooting opportunity. Use the laces or instep for power. Aim for the corners of the goal.

Progressions: Only pass using weaker foot. Only shoot using weaker foot. Introduce a defender to close down the attacker; the attacker may now take more than one touch to beat the defender.

››› 56 – 58 – 70 – 72

session 63 fast finish

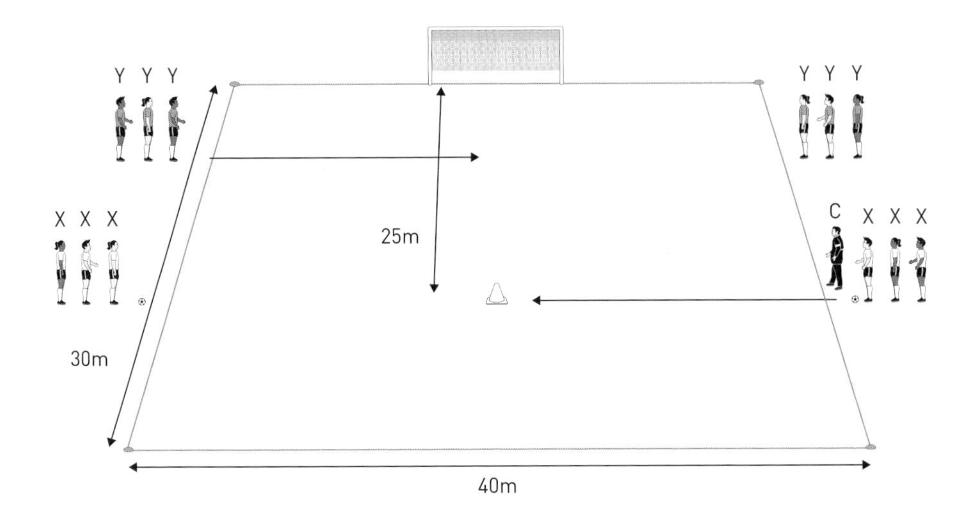

Organisation: Set up a 40 x 30 m area with a goal at one end. Split players into two equal teams, one attacking (X) and one defending (Y), on either side of the area. Players in the attacking team (X) need a ball at each of their start points. The defending team start closer to the goal. Mark out a cone in the centre of the area, 25 m from the goal.

Equipment: Goal, marker cones, traffic cone, bibs, footballs.

Description: The attacking players (X) start by running with the ball across the pitch to the central cone, then turning in to take a shot at goal. At the same time, a defender sprints across to the goal to attempt to block the shot. The next player from the attacking team then takes their turn against the next defender. The attacking team has three minutes to score as many times as they can, then swap roles with the defending team.

Key coaching points: Push the ball out of your feet when running with the ball to cover more ground. Turn quickly and sharply when you arrive at the centre cone. Use the laces or instep for power when shooting.

Progressions: After the turn, the attacker may only take one touch to shoot. Add a goalkeeper so that the attacker has to beat the defender and the keeper. Allow the defender to close down the attacker to create a 1 v 1.

››› 37 – 41 – 49 – 89

session 64 countdown

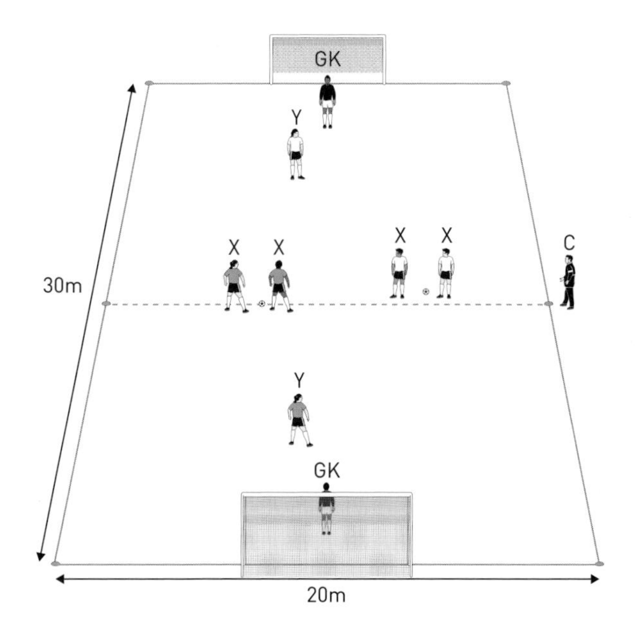

Organisation: Set out a 20 x 30m area with a goal at each end and a halfway line dividing the pitch into two sections. Organise the players into teams of four, with two attackers (X) on each team starting on the halfway line and the defending players set up with one as a goalkeeper (GK) and one defender (Y) in each half.

Equipment: Goals, marker cones, bibs, footballs.

Description: When the coach calls 'Go', the two attacking players (X) work together and attempt to score in the goal in their half of the area. The defending player (Y) and goalkeeper (GK) also work as a team to prevent them from scoring. The attackers are up against the clock, as they are given a 30-second countdown in which to score.

Key coaching points: Pass the ball quickly and be decisive in order to beat the clock. Use your pace and dribbling skills to beat the defender. Use the laces or instep for power when shooting.

Progressions: Offer bonus points for goals scored by a first time finish, a header or a volley. Reduce the amount of time to 20 seconds. Add an extra defender to create a 2 v 2.

››› 40 – 60 – 69 – 90

session 65 goal crazy

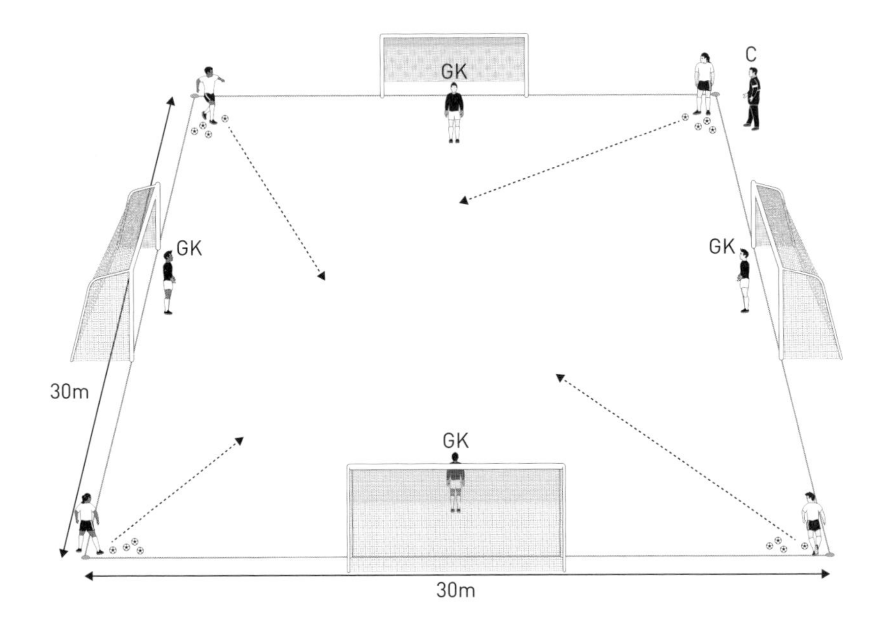

Organisation: Set out a 30 x 30m area with a goal on each side. Position a goalkeeper (GK) at each goal and one player in every corner with four footballs each.

Equipment: Goals, marker cones, bibs, footballs.

Description: When the coach calls 'Go', each player dribbles one of their footballs and attempts to score past any of the four goalkeepers. If they are successful, they get one point. Following the shot at goal, the attacker returns to their corner and collects another ball and attacks a different goal. Once all four players have had a shot at each of the four goals, the game is over and the player who scored the most goals wins. Rotate attackers and goalkeepers and repeat.

Key coaching points: Keep your head up and look around at the four goals when dribbling to see which one might be open for a shot. Use the laces or instep for power when shooting. Push the ball out of your feet when running with the ball to cover more ground.

Progressions: Offer bonus points for the fastest player to finish, encouraging quick play and decision making. Attackers must alternate taking shots with right foot and left foot. Add a defender to play against each attacker to create four 1 v 1 situations.

››› 28 – 42 – 63 – 91

session 66 shoot, head & volley

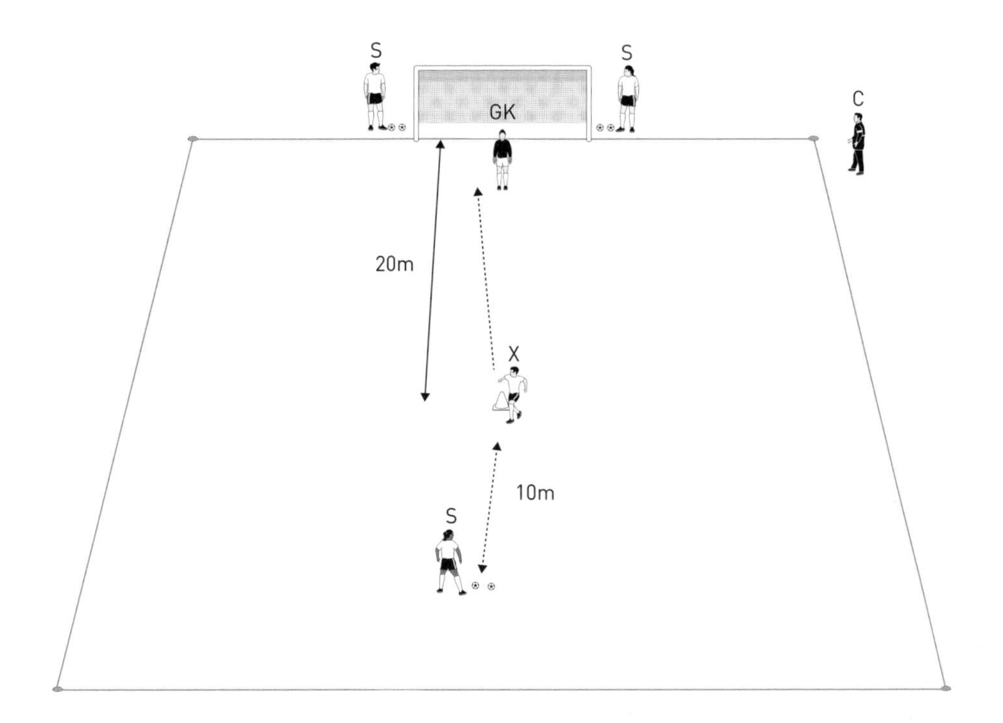

Organisation: Set out a traffic cone 20m in front of a goal. Set up with one attacking player (X) at the cone and three players as servers (S), with one each side of the goal and one in line with the attacking player, 10m away. The servers need two balls each. Add a goalkeeper (GK).

Equipment: Goal, marker cones, bibs, footballs.

Description: The servers (S) take turns in supplying the attacker (X) from their different positions with a different finish required each time. The first pass comes in with the attacker's back to goal so they have to turn and shoot in two touches. The second ball comes in from the left of the goal and has to be finished as a header. The final ball comes in from the right and has to be a volley. (The attacker is supplied two balls from each server, in sequence). Rotate players after each turn and keep score. The player that scores the most goals wins.

Key coaching points: The attacking player may move away from the traffic cone as they react to the supply, but must return to touch it before the next ball is played in to generate movement off the ball. Use the laces or instep for power when shooting. Keep your eye on the ball for the header and volleys, and try to get over the ball as you strike it.

Progressions: Only allow one touch to finish the shot, so that the attacker has to shoot on the turn. Attackers must alternate taking shots with right foot and left foot. Add a defender to play against each attacker to create three different 1 v 1 situations.

››› 50 – 59 – 70 – 79

session 67 back to goal

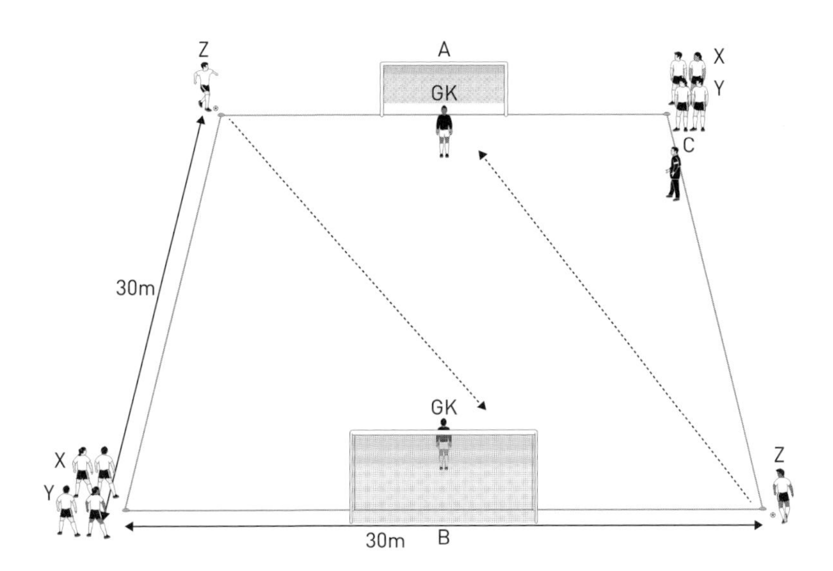

Organisation: Set out a 30 x 30m area with a goal at each end. The coach divides the players into two teams and positions them in opposite corners of the area as attackers (Y) and defenders (X). Two players act as servers (Z) and are placed in the two remaining corners.

Equipment: Goals, marker cones, bibs, football, traffic cones.

Description: The server (Z) passes the ball into the area towards the attacker (Y). The defender moves in front of the goal at their end in order to prevent a goal being scored, these players compete as a 1 v 1. If the defender wins the ball, they may attack the goal at the opposite end as a counter attack. Once a goal is scored or the attack is successfully defend that round is over and a ball is fed in from the other server to create a new 1 v 1.

Key coaching points: Rotate players so that they play in each of the roles. Play as a 2 v 2, but both players attacking player have to touch the ball on each side before they may take a shot on goal. Create a 2v1 defensive or attacking overload.

X team attempts to keep possession by creating space. Y team needs to win the ball then quickly counter attack.

Progressions: If the defender wins the ball, they and their opponent join the other pair at the other goal (2 v 2). The attacker dribbles onto the field with the defender behind him.

››› 33 – 58 – 62 – 93

session 68 shoot solo

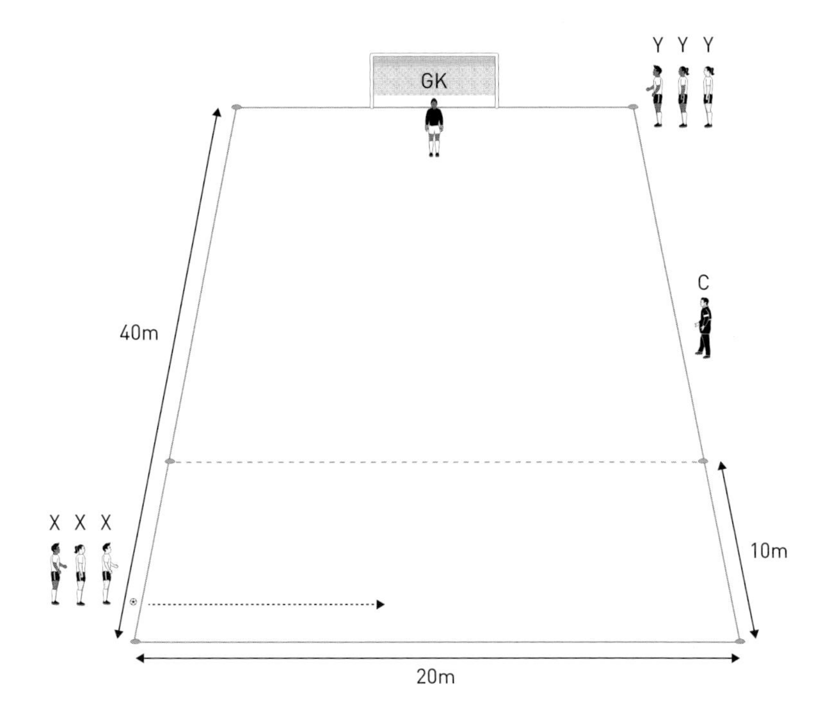

Organisation: Set out a 20 x 40m area with a goal at one end and a 20 x 10m area at the other end with 3 v 3 situation.

Equipment: Goal, marker cones, bibs, football.

Description: The objective is to dribble across the inside end line and score. If an attacker dribbles across the inside end line, they can shoot without interference. After the shot, regardless of the result, the player and their teammates start an attack on the outside end line. If an attacker dribbles across this line, their team keeps the ball and begins another attack in the opposite direction.

Key coaching points: X team attempt to keep possession by creating space. Y team need to win the ball then quickly counter attack.

Progression: Increase to 4 v 4.

››› 25 – 52 – 61 – 80

session 69 shot race

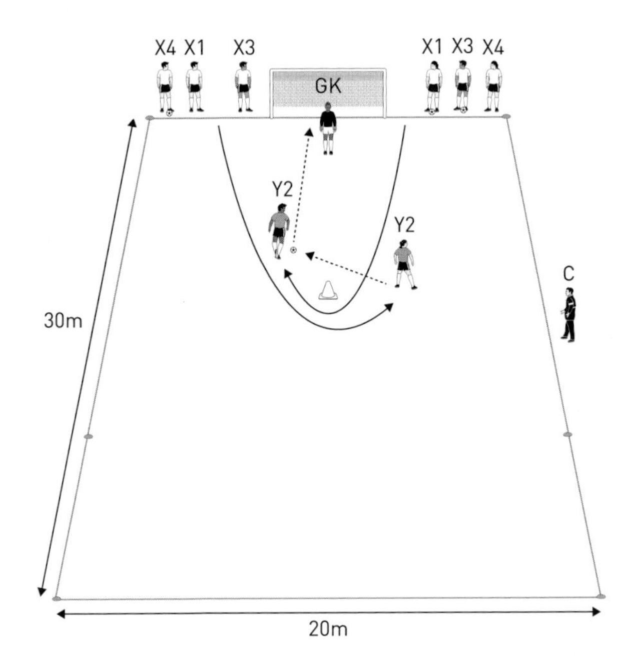

Organisation: Set out a 30 x 20m area with one goal.

Equipment: Goal, marker cones, bibs, footballs, traffic cone.

Description: The players divide into pairs. Each pair has a ball. One player (X) in each pair stands to the left of the goal, the other (Y) stands to the right. The players both pass their ball in front of goal then run around the traffic cones at top speed. The first player to reach their ball can shoot. Which player can score most goals?

Key coaching points: Improve sprinting. Practise early shooting. Adapting quickly.

Progression: Both players must run through a slalom on the way to their balls. Both players can shoot after racing to their balls; the player who first reaches their ball shoots first and their opponent must wait until they're done before they can shoot too. Both players can shoot after racing to their balls, but the second attacker shoots against a second goalkeeper, who starts from behind the goal.

››› 53 – 54 – 64 – 88

session 70 two-touch finishing

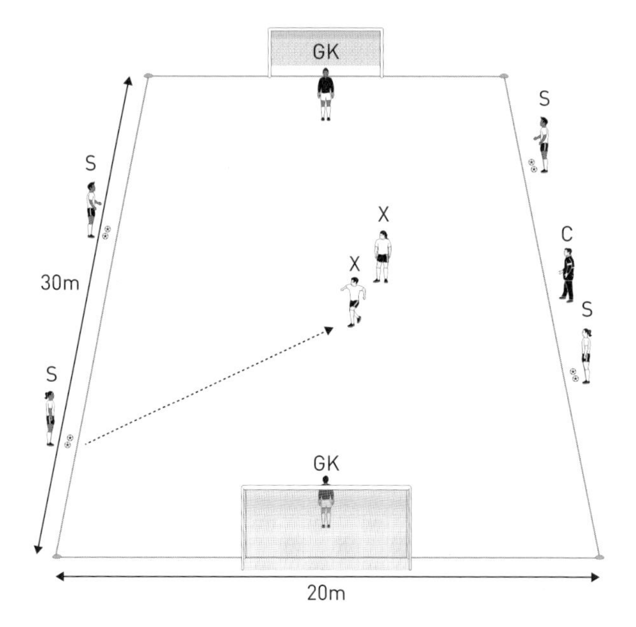

Organisation: Set out a 20 x 30m area with a goal at each end and a goalkeeper (GK) in each goal. Organise players into pairs, with two pairs acting as servers (S) and two as strikers (X). Each of the serving players needs two balls each.

Equipment: Goals, marker cones, bibs, footballs.

Description: The servers (S) take turns in supplying the attackers from their different positions. As the ball comes in to the attacking pair (X), they have two touches (one each) to score in either of the goals. One player must provide the set-up and the other must try to finish. Rotate after all the servers have played each of their footballs into the area and keep score to see which pair are the best strike partners.

Key coaching points: Communicate and work as a pair. Cushion the ball into space to set up a shot for your partner. Use the laces or instep for power when shooting.

Progressions: Servers chip the ball into the area to make the first touch more difficult to control. Attackers must alternate taking shots with right foot and left foot. Add a defender to play against each attacker to create a 2 v 1 situations (allow the attackers extra touches if necessary).

››› 48 – 50 – 66 – 81

SMALL-SIDED GAMES

Small-sided games are a developmentally appropriate environment for young players to learn and improve. Each game incorporates a specific football technique such as dribbling, passing or shooting, or focuses on team play and strategies such as defending, attacking, creating space or switching play.

These games are designed to bring the best out of players in realistic match situations. By allowing the players to enjoy more playing time, their understanding of the importance of team play, relative positional sense and decision making will be greatly improved.

session 71 corner cones

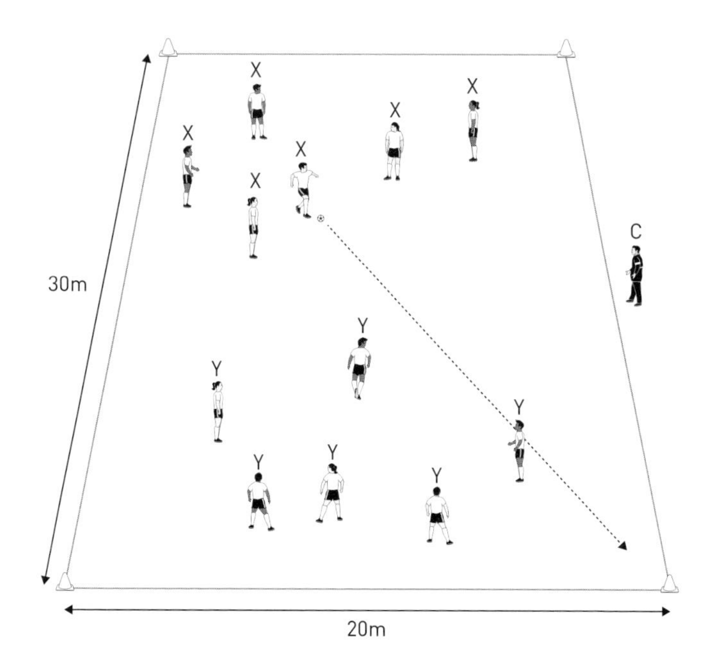

Organisation: Set out a 20 x 30m area with a traffic cone in each corner. Organise the players into two teams of no more than 6 v 6.

Equipment: Traffic cones, bibs, football.

Description: The teams attempt to score points by passing the ball and knocking down the traffic cones in the corners of the area, but can only attack the two cones in the opposite corners of the area.

Key coaching points: Pass to your teammates to create space for an attempt at goal. Use the inside of the foot to pass. Go for goal as soon as an opportunity arises.

Progressions: Only score using weaker foot. Only score with a first-time pass. Play attacking end to end as opposed to attacking the opposite corners.

››› 57 – 60– 66 – 75

session 72 counter attack

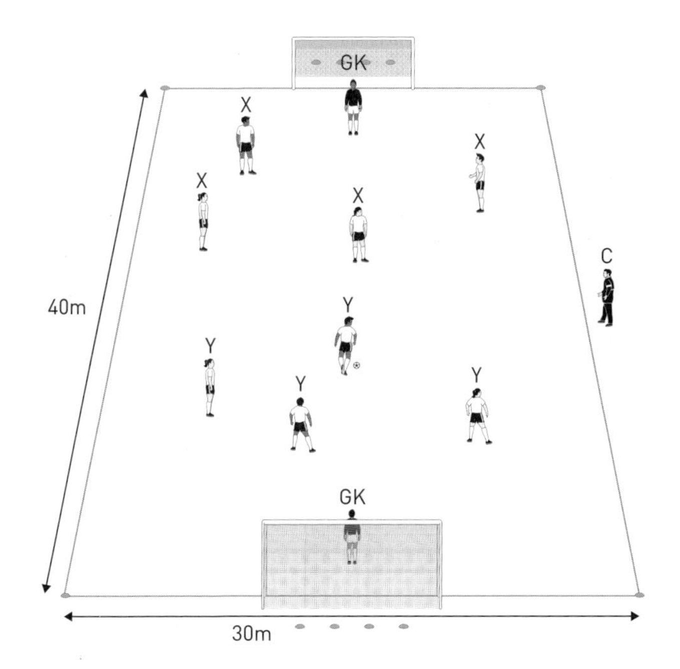

Organisation: Set out a 40 x 30m area with four small cones placed behind each goal. Organise the players into two teams of 4 v 4 plus two goalkeepers (GK).

Equipment: Goals, marker cones, bibs, football.

Description: The teams play 4 v 4 inside the area. When a player scores a goal, they must run to retrieve one cone from behind the goal and place behind their own goal. This player may not touch the ball again until the cone is placed behind their goal, creating the opportunity for the opposition to counter attack with a 4 v 3 overload. The team with the most cones after ten minutes of play wins.

Key coaching points: Can the team that concedes counter attack quickly? Can the defending team organise themselves efficiently enough to not concede before their player returns to the game?

Progressions: Only score using weaker foot. Only score with a first-time finish. Limit players to no more the two or three touches each time they receive the ball.

››› 40 – 53 – 64 – 90

session 73 attack v defence overload

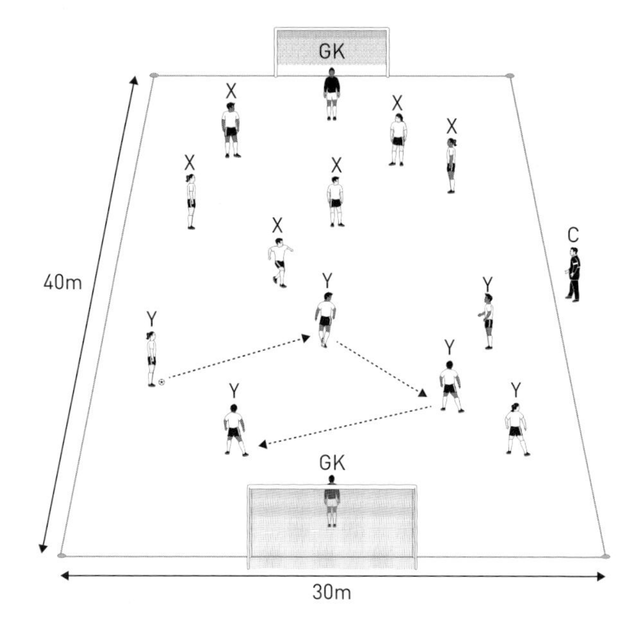

Organisation: Set out a 30 x 40m area with a goal at each end. Organise the players into 6 v 6 with two additional goalkeepers (GK).

Equipment: Goals, marker cones, bibs, football.

Description: The teams (X and Y) play 6 v 6 inside the area in an attack vs. defence practice. The goalkeepers both play on the defending team, to create an 8 v 6 overload. The objective for the defenders is to make ten passes to score a point. The objective for the attackers is to win the ball back and then score in either of the goals. Each phase of play starts with the defending team so that the attackers have to win the ball back.

Key coaching points: Attacking team wins the ball and counter attacks quickly. Defenders work as a team to keep possession. Goalkeeper is only allowed to use their feet when their team is in possession, developing footwork and passing ability.

Progression: Limit players to no more the two or three touches each time they receive the ball. Only score with a first-time finish. Only score with weaker foot.

››› 48 – 58 – 69 – 95

session 74 tiki-taka

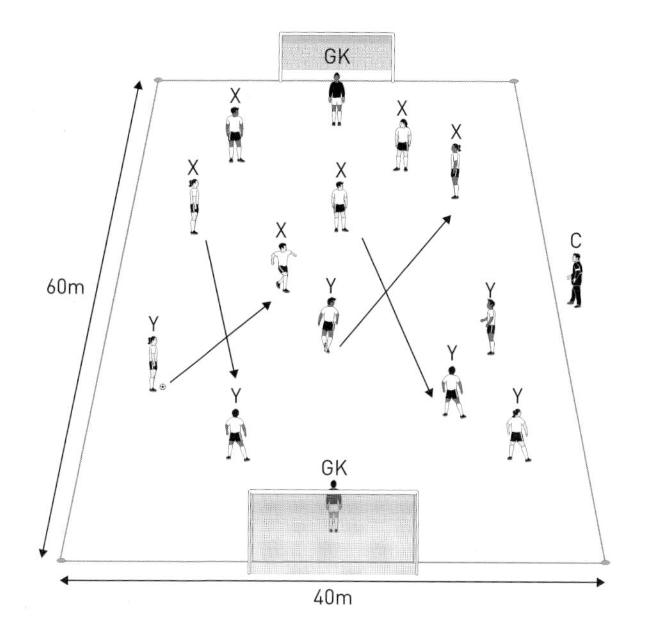

Organisation: Set out a 40 x 60m area with a goal at each end. Organise the players into 6 v 6 plus two goalkeepers (GK).

Equipment: Goals, marker cones, bibs, football.

Description: The teams play 6 v 6 inside the area in a normal match practice attempting to score in the opposition's goal. When the coach calls out 'Tiki-Taka' neither team may score, and the aim is to keep possession of the ball. Play for three minutes, and when the time elapses whichever team is in possession of the ball scores a point. Return to normal match play and repeat.

Key coaching points: Work as a team to keep possession. Can you create space to receive a pass from your teammate? Work to close down the opposition when not in possession.

Progressions: Limit players to no more the two or three touches each time they receive the ball. Award a bonus point if a team manages more than ten passes without losing possession.

››› 56 – 59 – 70 – 72

session 75 goals v targets

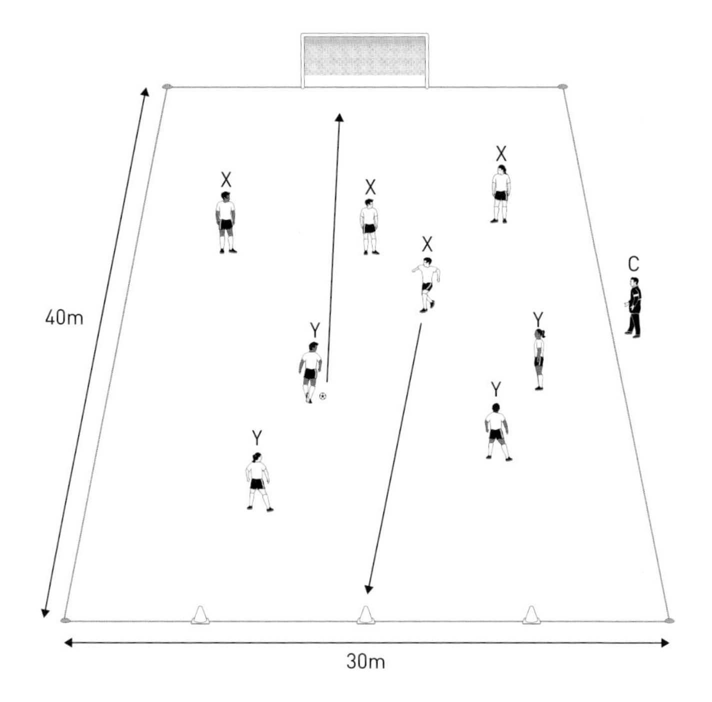

Organisation: Set out a 30 x 40m area with a goal at one end and two target goals at the opposite end. The target goals are created by using three traffic cones lined up together. Organise the players into 4 v 4.

Equipment: Marker cones, bibs, a football.

Description: The teams play 4 v 4 inside the area with one team attacking the goal and the other team attacking the target goal – attempting to score by hitting the traffic cones and knocking them over. Whenever a goal is scored the teams change ends, thereby changing the way they score a goal and their team's objective.

Key coaching points: Pass to your teammates to create space for an attempt at goal. Can the team attacking the target goals attempt to switch play? Go for goal as soon as an opportunity arises.

Progressions: Reduce target goal to two cones on each side to make it harder to score. Limit players to no more the two or three touches each time they receive the ball. Only score with a first-time finish.

››› 42 – 57 – 68 – 71

session 76 rugby football

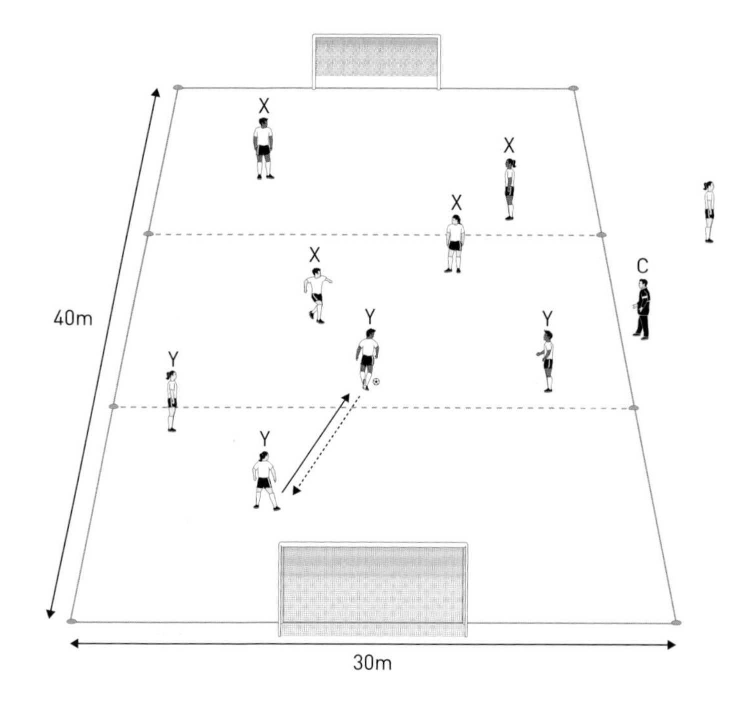

Organisation: Set out a 30 x 40m area with a goal at each end and two lines dividing the area into three equal thirds.

Equipment: Goals, marker cones, bibs, football.

Description: The teams play 4 v 4 inside the area aiming to score against the opposition but the players are not allowed to pass the ball forwards. They must dribble forward in order to attack the opposition goal but are only permitted to pass backwards. A goal can only be scored when inside the attacking third of the pitch.

Key coaching points: Encourage players to dribble at the defenders and use their skills to beat them. Support the play from behind. Communication.

Progressions: Allow teams to score from the central third, but only if it's a first-time shot. Award bonus points for good skills. May only score if you have dribbled past a defender.

››› 30 – 53 – 66 – 101

session 77 corner ball

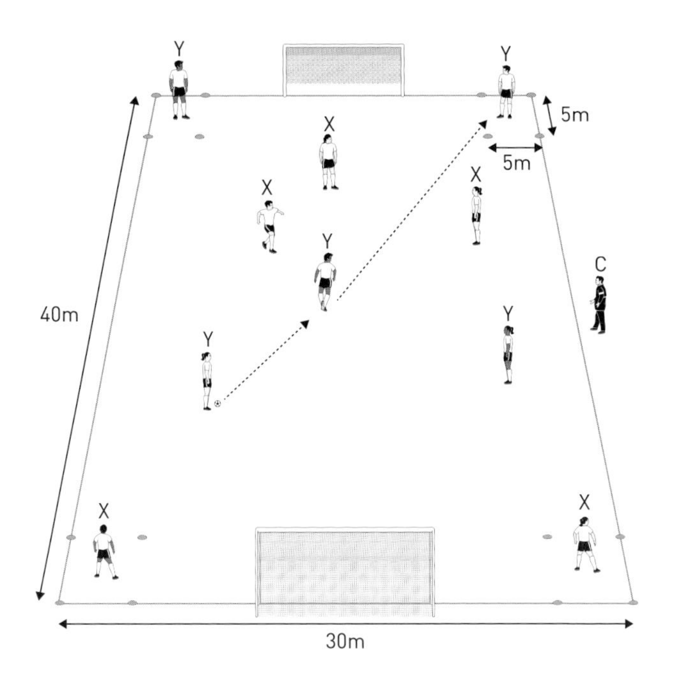

Organisation: Set out a 30 x 40m area with a goal at each end and four 5 x 5m target areas, one in each corner. Organise players into teams of five with a 3 v 3 in the main area and the other two players from each team in the corner target areas.

Equipment: Goals, marker cones, bibs, football.

Description: The teams play 3 v 3 inside the area and attempt to score a goal by passing into their target areas so that their teammate can control the ball. The player that played in the pass then becomes the target player. If they make a successful pass in and out of the corner, they score one point. If they score a goal, it's two points, but if they make a successful pass in and out of the corner and then score a goal without losing possession, it counts as five points.

Key coaching points: Accurate pass into target player. Work as a team to keep possession. Use the corner players to create an overload.

Progressions: Can only score by dribbling into the area and the target player dribbling it out. Can only score after playing a 1–2 with one of the support players. Ball must be chipped into the target area for the target player to catch.

››› 51 – 58 – 61 – 83

session 78 limited touch zones

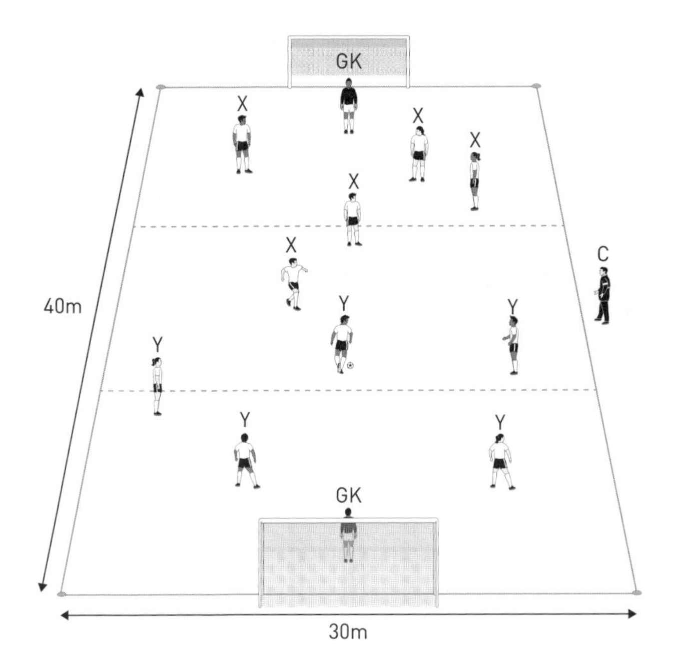

Organisation: Set out a 30 x 40m area divided into three equal sections, creating two end zones and a midfield zone, and a goal at each end. Organise players into teams of five with a goalkeeper (GK) in each goal.

Equipment: Goals, marker cones, bibs, football.

Description: The teams play 5 v 5 inside the area and are limited to the amount of touches they can take on the ball depending on which zone they are in. All players have unlimited touches in the end zones but can only play three touches in the midfield zone.

Key coaching points: Move the ball quickly through the zones to set up a scoring opportunity. Work as a team to support in the limited touch zone to keep possession.

Progression: Play one touch in the midfield zones.

››› 35 – 48 – 48 – 91

session 79 diagonal goals

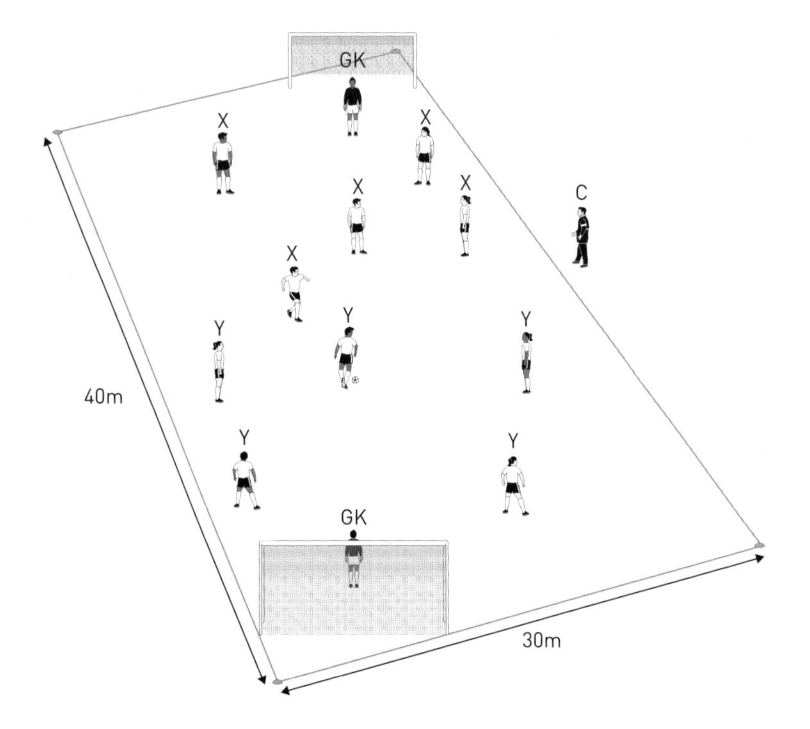

Organisation: Set out a 30 x 40m area with a goal placed in two opposite corners. Organise players into 5 v 5 with a goalkeeper (GK) each.

Equipment: Goals, marker cones, bibs, football.

Description: The teams play 5 v 5, attempting to score in the other team's goal, which is placed in the corner of the area, changing the angles of attack.

Key coaching points: Encourage players to be on the half turn so are able to see and play in both directions. Work as a team to keep possession.

Progressions: Add a small gate in the middle of the area which teams have to play through before they attack the goal. First-time finish only to encourage build-up play in attack.

››› 44 – 53 – 65 – 92

session 80 snookered

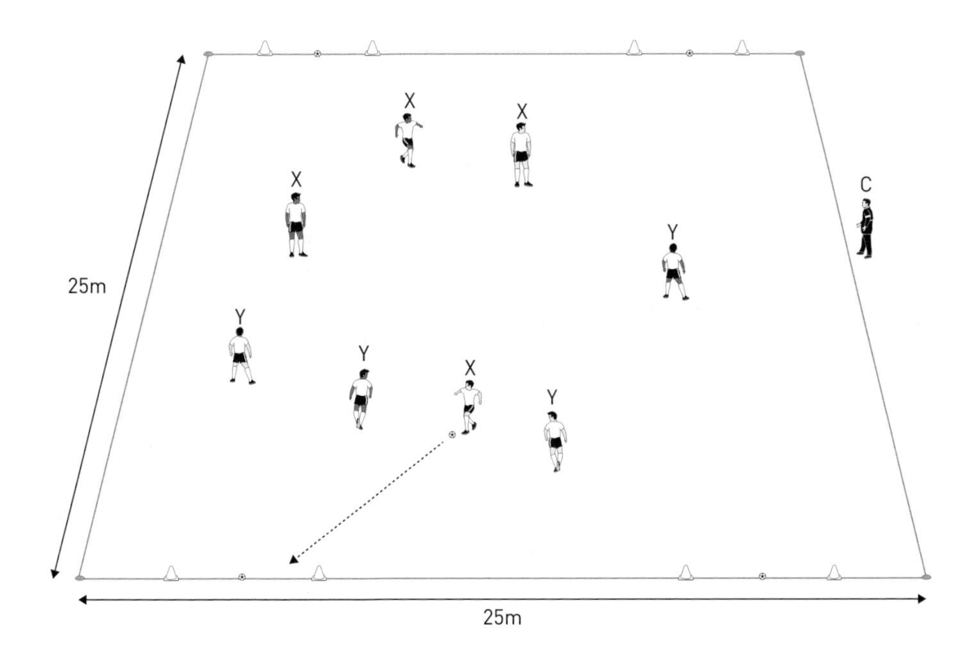

Organisation: Set out a 25 x 25m area with four small goals in each corner. Place a football on the goal line of each of the four small goals. Organise the players into 4 v 4.

Equipment: Traffic cones, marker cones, bibs, football.

Description: The teams play 4 v 4 inside the area with one team attacking two goals at one end and the other team attacking the other two goals. Players score one point for passing the ball into the small goal or three points for playing the match ball onto the ball on the goal line and knocking it into the goal – just like snooker!

Key coaching points: Pass to your teammates to create space for an attempt at goal. If one small goal is being defended, can you switch play? Accurate passing to score extra points.

Progressions: Teams change from attacking end to end to diagonally opposite goals. Limit players to no more than two or three touches each time they receive the ball. Team can accumulate points per passes with a point per pass, so five passes and a 'snooker' goal equals eight points.

››› 38 – 51 – 65 – 85

session 81 ten-pass total football

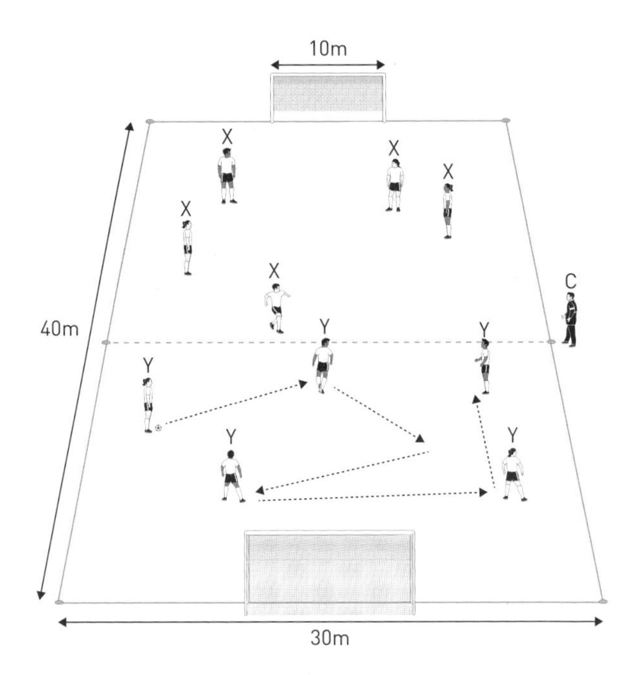

Organisation: Set out a 30 x 40m area with a large (10m) goal at each end marked out with traffic cones (or use a full-sized goal). Split the area into two halves and organise the players into 4 v 4, with one team in each half.

Equipment: Goals (or traffic cones), marker cones, bibs, football.

Description: One team starts with the ball and make five 'free' passes under no pressure, in their own half. After the fifth pass, a player from the opposing team may enter their half and apply pressure. If they successfully make it to ten passes, they can attempt to score by shooting from inside their own half with a first-time shot, or by advancing as a team into the defending team's half to get closer to the goal.

Key coaching points: Aim to switch play to score in a less well-defended goal. Work as a team to attack and defend the goals as you win and lose possession. Aim for the corners of the goal when shooting.

Progressions: Limit players to no more than two or three touches each time they receive the ball. Only score with a first-time finish inside the opponent's half. Only score with a header or volley inside the opponent's half.

››› 46 – 66 – 67 – 93

session 82 floating keepers

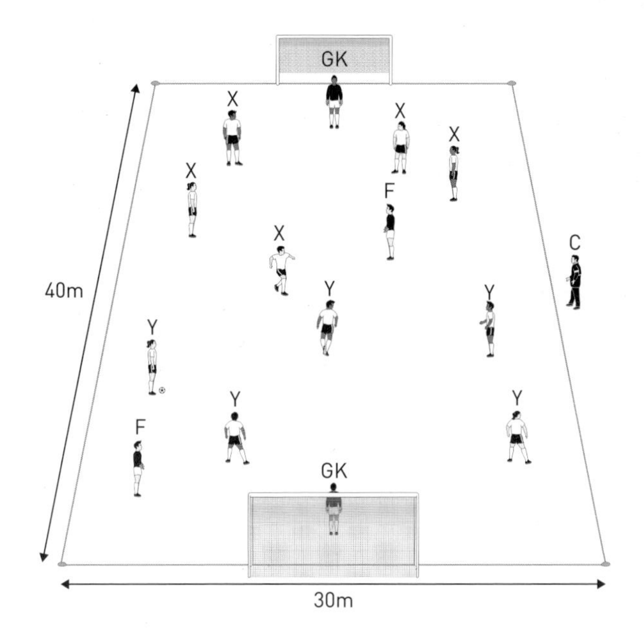

Organisation: Set out a 30 x 40m area with a goal at each end. Organise the teams into two teams of 5 v 5 with two goalkeepers (GK) and an additional two floating keepers (F).

Equipment: Goals, marker cones, bibs, football.

Description: Each team starts with a goalkeeper (GK) in their goal and a floating keeper (F) that can move around the pitch with the rest of the players. The floating keeper is allowed to use their hands or their feet in any area of the field, but may not score using their hands or move when they have the ball in their hands.

Key coaching points: Focus on goalkeeper distribution from hands. Floating goalkeepers aim to set up shots at goal by rolling or throwing the ball to players in space. Goalkeepers in goal aim to set up fast break attacks with quick distribution.

Progressions: Limit floating goalkeepers to three seconds with the ball in their hands. On the coaches call, the two keepers swap roles during the game. Only score from a direct set-up from the floating keeper.

››› 50 – 59 – 66 – 88

session 83 snooze soccer

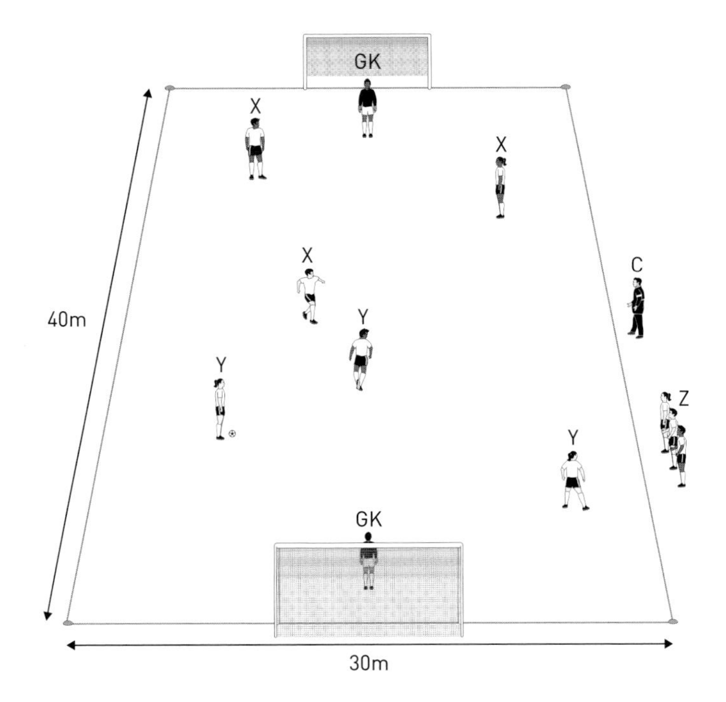

Organisation: Set out a 40 x 30m area with a goal at each end. Each goal has a permanent goalkeeper. Divide the group into three teams.

Equipment: Goals, marker cones, bibs, football.

Description: At any given time, two teams (X and Y) play freely in the area while the third team (Z) rests outside the area. Whenever a team scores, their opponents leave the area and the resting team come into play. The team that scored keeps the ball, switches direction, and attacks against the new team. The resting team must pay close attention to the game in order to get on the field as soon as their turn comes up! If no team has scored after two minutes, the team that's been playing longer must leave. Which team can score the most goals?

Key coaching points: X team attempts to keep possession by creating space. Y team needs to win the ball by creating pressure and closing down space. Speed of action.

Progression: Remove the 'permanent' goalkeepers.

››› 28 – 53 – 61 – 77

session 84 3 v 3 cover your goal

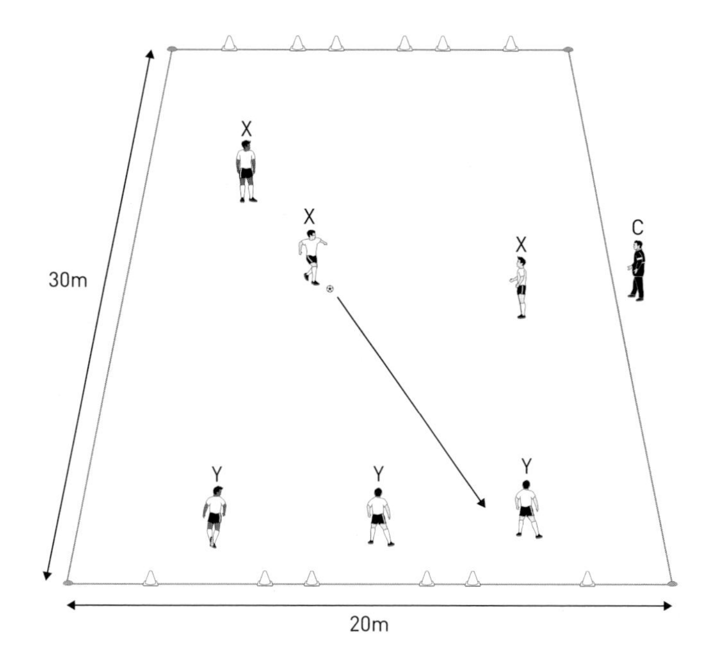

Organisation: Set out a 20 x 30m area with three small goals at each end. Divide the group into teams of three.

Equipment: Traffic cones, marker cones, bibs, football.

Description: The teams play 3 v 3 inside the area attempting to score by passing the ball into any of the three goals. In attack, any X player can score in any goal. When defending, a Y player is responsible for covering a particular goal. Only that player is allowed to defend that goal.

Key coaching points: If your goal isn't being attacked, apply pressure to try to win the ball back. If you lose possession up-field, try to regroup and cover your goal as quickly as possible.

Progressions: Limit players to one goal to attack and one to defend. Limit players to a first-time finish to encourage build-up play in attack.

››› 44 – 60 – 68 – 97

session 85 quick-pass corners

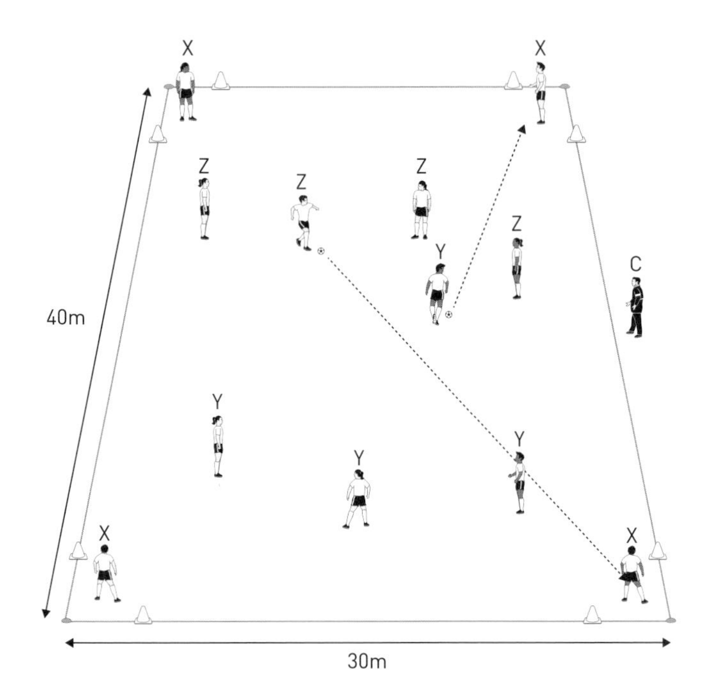

Organisation: Set out a 40 x 30m area with four small gates, diagonally across each corner. Organise players into three teams of four with one team (X) standing in each corner of the area.

Equipment: Traffic cones, marker cones bibs, football.

Description: The teams (Y and Z) play 4 v 4 inside the area attempting to score by passing the ball to any of the four corner players (X) and receiving it back as a 1–2. Teams may not score in the same goal twice in succession.

Key coaching points: Accurate passes into the corner, then move to be in a space ready to receive the return pass. If the corner you are attacking is being defended, switch the play to attack a different goal.

Progressions: Teams only attack and defend two goals in opposite corners. Teams only attack and defend two goals end to end.

>>> 55 – 60 – 70 – 83

session 86 two zones

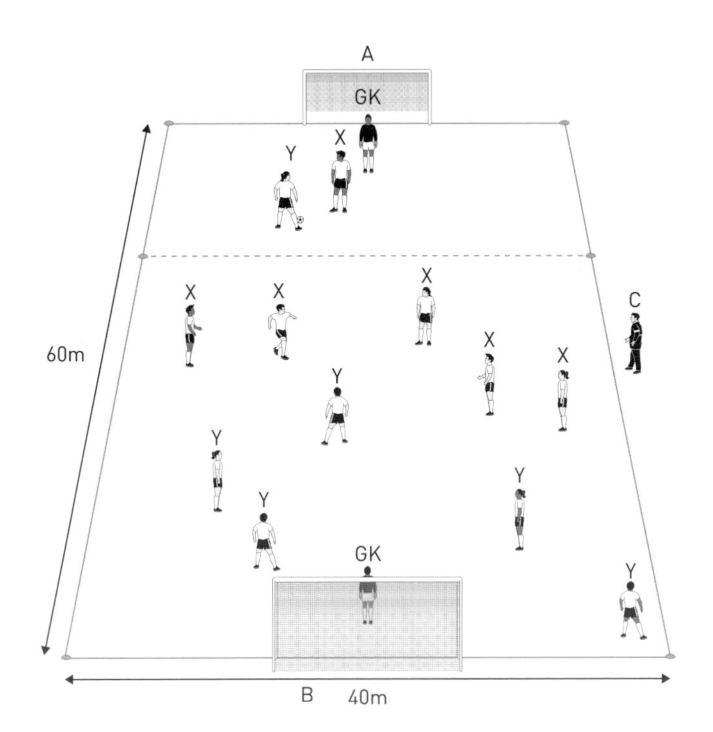

Organisation: Set out a 40 x 60m area with the area divided into two unequal zones which are marked with cones. Create two teams of six, distributed as follows: 5 v 5 in the large zone in front of a goal, 1 v 1 in the other zone in front of another goal. Both goals have goalkeepers (GK).

Equipment: Goals, marker cones, bibs, football.

Description: Players may not leave their assigned zones, with one exception: If the X team (defending goal A) wins the ball and successfully passes it to its forward in the small zone, they may send one additional player over the line to create a 2 v 1.

Key coaching points: Create space. Communication. First touch. Movement. Execution of pass and shot.

Progressions: 4 v 4 and 2 v 2. Whenever team X sends an attacker across the line, Y team can send an extra defender. All players must stay in their assigned zones at all times.

>>> 25 – 53 – 61 – 94

session 87 set piece soccer

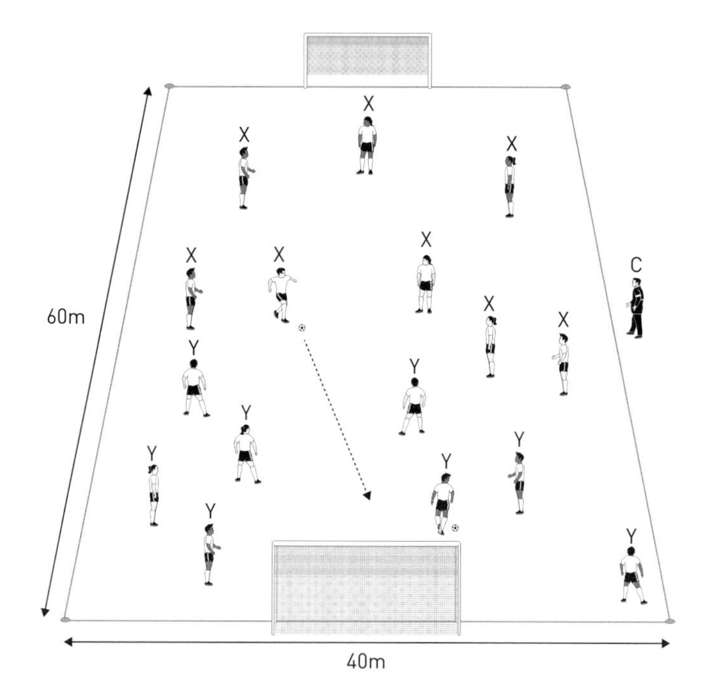

Organisation: Set out a 60 x 40m area, with a goal at each end. Organise the players into 8 v 8.

Equipment: Goals, marker cones, bibs, football.

Description: Play 8 v 8. For each shot on goal, regardless of whether it scores, the attackers get a corner kick. If the ball goes out of touch, play resumes with a free kick instead of a throw-in.

Key coaching points: Create space. Communication. First touch. Movement. Execution of pass and shot.

Progressions: All players are limited to two or three touches. Attackers get two corner kicks for each shot on goal. Make the area larger or smaller.

››› 50 – 56 – 66 – 98

session 88 over the wall

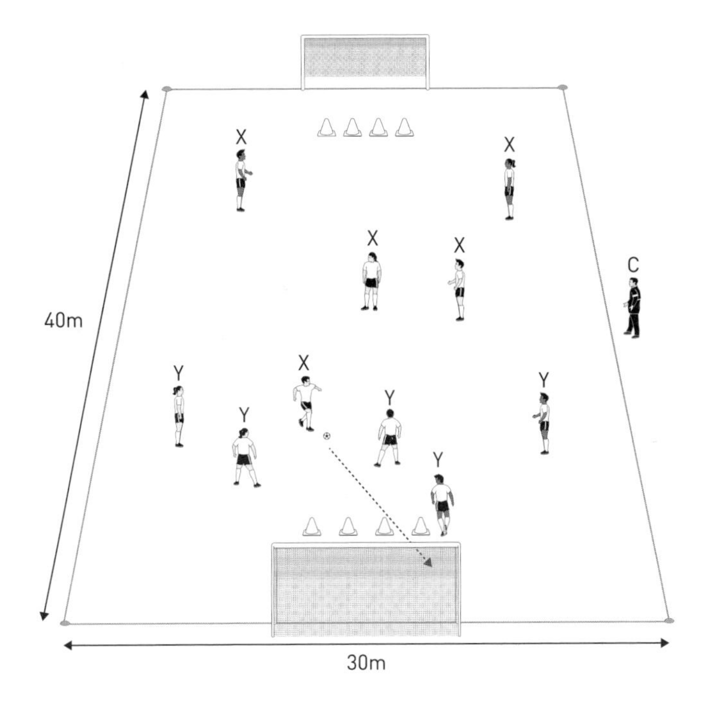

Organisation: Set out a 30 x 40m area with a five-a-side goal at each end. Place a row of 4 traffic cones in front of each goal to create a 'wall'. Organise the players into 5 v 5.

Equipment: Goals, marker cones, bibs, football, traffic cones.

Description: The teams play 5 v 5 inside the area without goalkeepers. In order to score a goal, the players must shoot from inside the opposition's half and into the goal without hitting or knocking down any of the traffic cones. If they knock down part of the wall, the goal does not count. The first team to three goals wins.

Key coaching points: Aim for the corners of the goal. Try to chip the ball over the wall but under the crossbar. Go for goal as soon as an opportunity arises.

Progressions: Allow players to shoot from anywhere on the pitch. Limit players to no more the two or three touches each time they receive the ball. Only score with a first-time finish.

››› 57 – 58 – 68 – 82

session 89 four goal 4 v 4

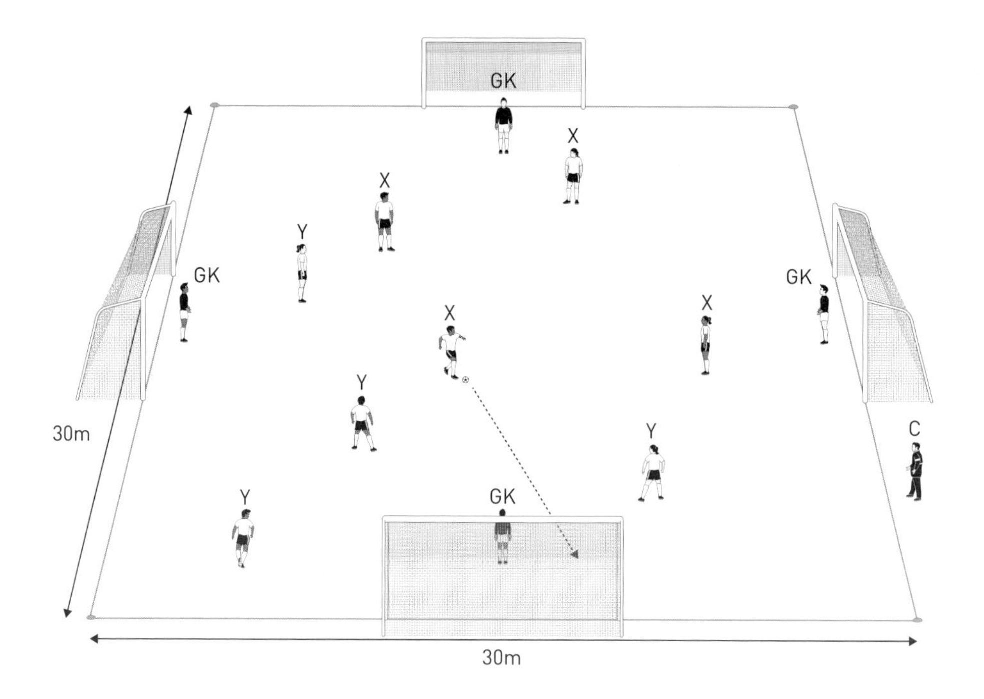

Organisation: Set out a 30 x 30m area with a five-a-side goal (or traffic cones) on each side of the area. Organise the players into 4 v 4, and add a goalkeeper (GK) in each goal.

Equipment: Goals or traffic cones, marker cones, bibs, football.

Description: The teams play 4 v 4 inside the area and attempt to win the game by scoring once in each of the four goals. When a team scores, that goal is then 'closed' and they aim to score in one of the other three, and continue until they have managed to score in all four.

Key coaching points: Aim to switch play to score in a less-defended goal. Work as a team to attack and defend the goals as you win and lose possession. Aim for the corners of the goal when shooting.

Progressions: Open up all goals at all times (even if already scored in), but add a time limit to see which team can score the most goals. Limit players to no more the two or three touches each time they receive the ball. Only score with a first-time finish.

››› **25 – 47 – 54 – 100**

session 90 collect & attack

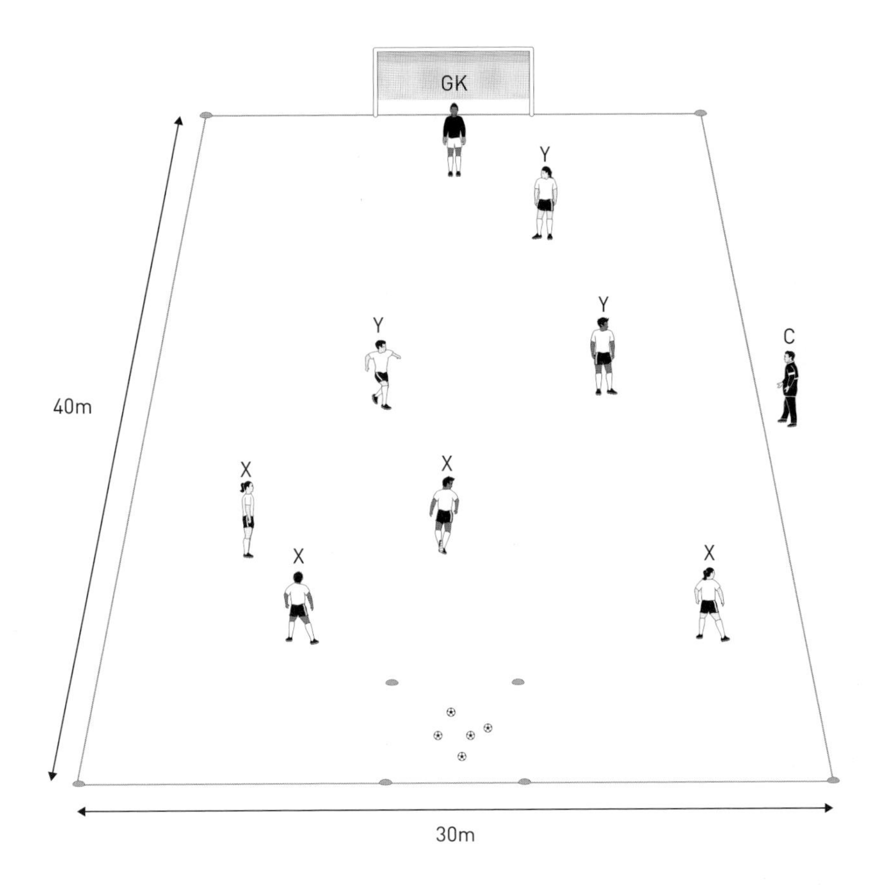

Organisation: Set out a 40 x 30m area with a goal at one end. Organise the players into 4 v 4. The defending team needs to set up with a goalkeeper (GK) in the goal and three outfield defenders. Set up five footballs in a marked square at the end of the area.

Equipment: Goal, marker cones, bibs, football.

Description: The teams play 4 v 3 inside the area with the team of 4 attacking and the team of 3 defending. The attacking team have five attempts to scores as many goals as they can by collecting a ball from the square and attacking the goal. If the ball is successfully defended (cleared or dribbled out of play), they retrieve another ball and go again until all the balls are gone. Each goal scores one point for that team. Once all the balls are finished they switch roles.

Key coaching points: Use the man advantage to work as a team and create space for shooting opportunities. Defend as a unit to try to restrict space for the attacking team. Go for goal as soon as an opportunity arises.

Progressions: Allow the defending team to win a bonus point if they are able to stop the ball in the square. Limit players to no more than two or three touches each time they receive the ball. Add a time limit per ball to apply pressure to the attacking team.

››› 25 – 40 – 64 – 72

session 91 time team

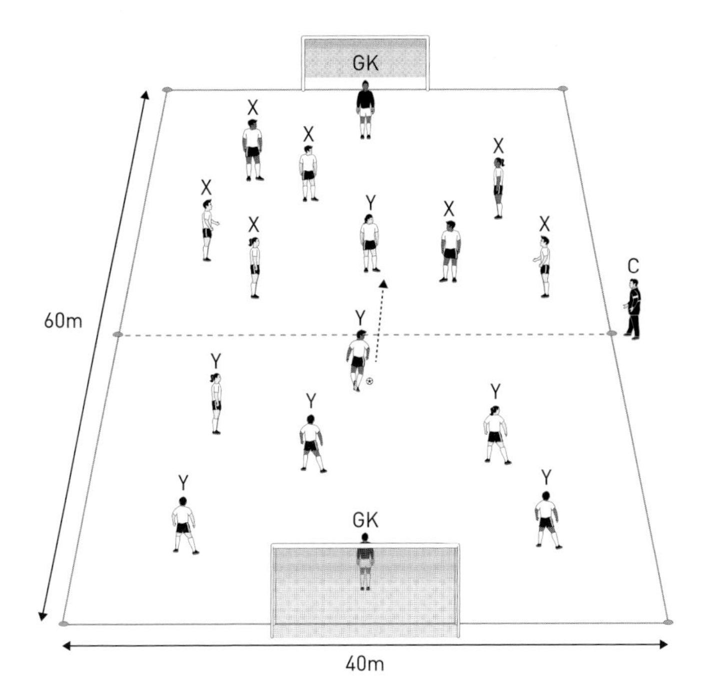

Organisation: Set out a 40 x 60m area with a goal at each end and a halfway line dividing the area into two equal sections. Organise players into two teams of eight.

Equipment: Goals, marker cones, bibs, football.

Description: Once a defender wins the ball, they must pass it to their teammates in the other half, who then tries to score. Attackers only have 10 seconds to shoot, or they lose the ball.

Key coaching points: Create space. Communication. First touch. Movement. Execution of pass and shot.

Progressions: Overload the defending team. Make the area larger or smaller. Decrease the time limit allowed for players to take their shot at goal.

››› **47 – 64 – 68 – 81**

session 92 man marking

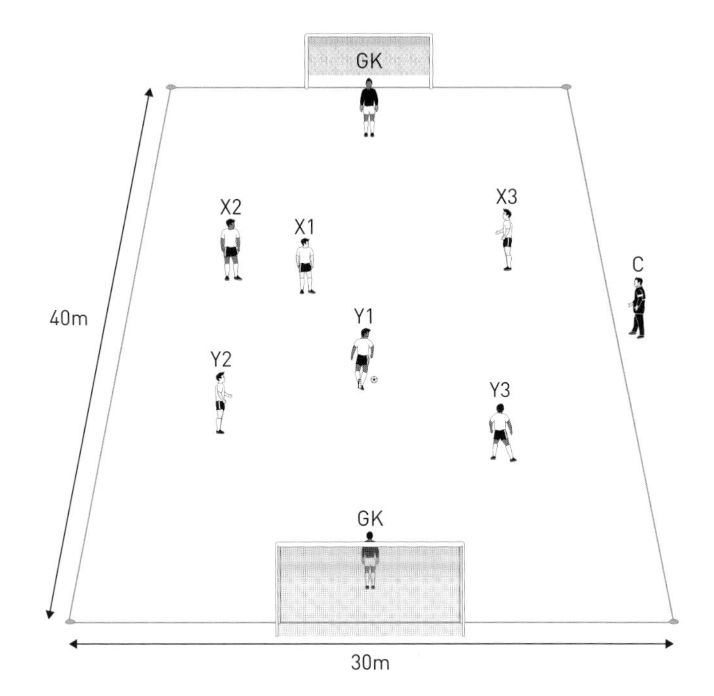

Organisation: Set out a 30 x 40 m area with a goal at each end. Organise the players into teams of five, with a goalkeeper each.

Equipment: Goals, marker cones, bibs, football.

Description: Teams play 5 v 5 with each player matched up against a player from the opposition. It is each player's job to ensure that their direct opponent does not score a goal.

Key coaching points: Work hard to lose your marker. Stick with your opponent in attack and defence.

Progression: Add a floating player who plays for whichever team has possession but cannot score and is limited to three touches each time they receive the ball. Limit all players to three touches. Introduce a forfeit for any defender who lets their opponent score.

››› 22 – 24 – 61 – 79

session 93 centre goal

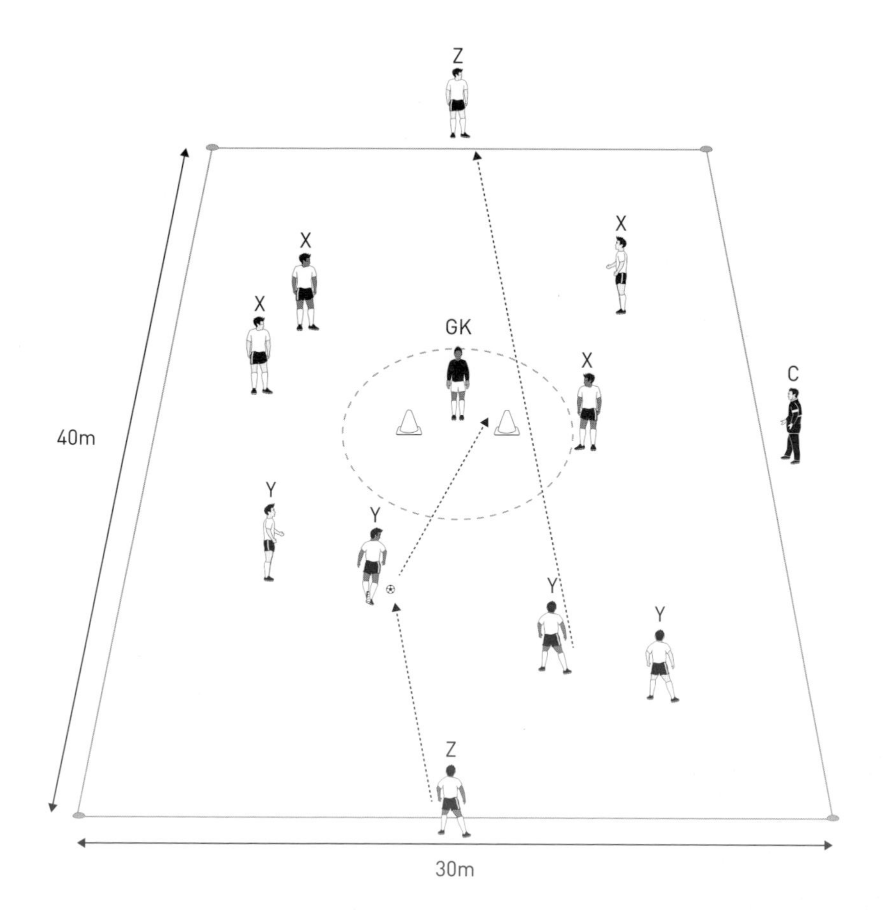

Organisation: Set out a 30 x 40m area with a goal placed in the middle using traffic cones. Mark a circle area around the goal which is the 'goalkeeper zone'. The centre circle is an ideal space for this game. Organise the players into two teams of four, with a support player (Z) for each team on their baseline, and a goalkeeper (GK) in the circle who is neutral.

Equipment: Traffic cones, marker cones, bibs, football.

Description: Teams play 4 v 4 and are allowed to score from either side of the goal but before either team can take a shot on goal they must play a 1-2 with their support player (Z) in order to build the attack. Players are allowed to move anywhere inside the area but cannot score from inside the goalkeeper zone.

Key coaching points: Go for goal as soon as an opportunity arises. Be alive to rebounds or missed shots as the game will continue after each shot, successful or not.

Progressions: Add an extra support player from each team on both of the baselines so that players can develop attacks from either end. Allow the support player to join the game once they have played a 1–2 to create an overload.

››› 57 – 65 – 70 – 81

session 94 join the attack

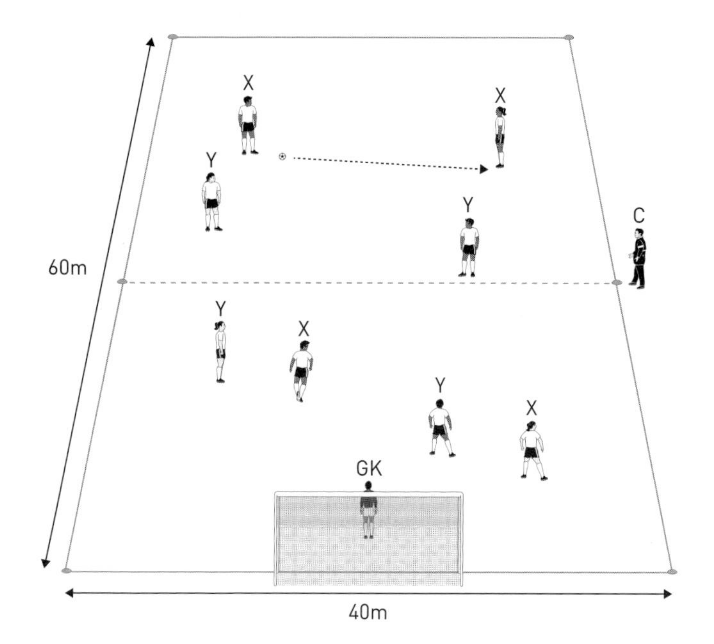

Organisation: Set out a 40 x 60m area, divided into two 40 x 30m areas (midfield and attack v defence) with a goal at one end. Organise teams into 4 v 4 with one goalkeeper (GK), and split them into a 2 v 2 in each of the two areas.

Equipment: Goal, marker cones, bibs, football.

Description: The ball starts in the 'midfield' area with the 2 v 2. Players attempt to win possession and pass into the 'attack v defence' area. Whichever team manages to play the ball into the area is then able to play 2 v 2 and tries to score while the other team become defenders and attempt to stop them.

Key coaching points: X team attempt to keep possession by creating space. Y team need to win the ball then quickly counter attack.

Progressions: The midfield 2 v 2 must make three passes between them before the ball can be passed into the attacking zone. Players may only score with a first-time finish. Allow the player that passes into the attacking third to join the attack to create a 3 v 2 overload. Players must stay in their designated area.

››› 30 – 52 – 69 – 86

session 95 goals v passes

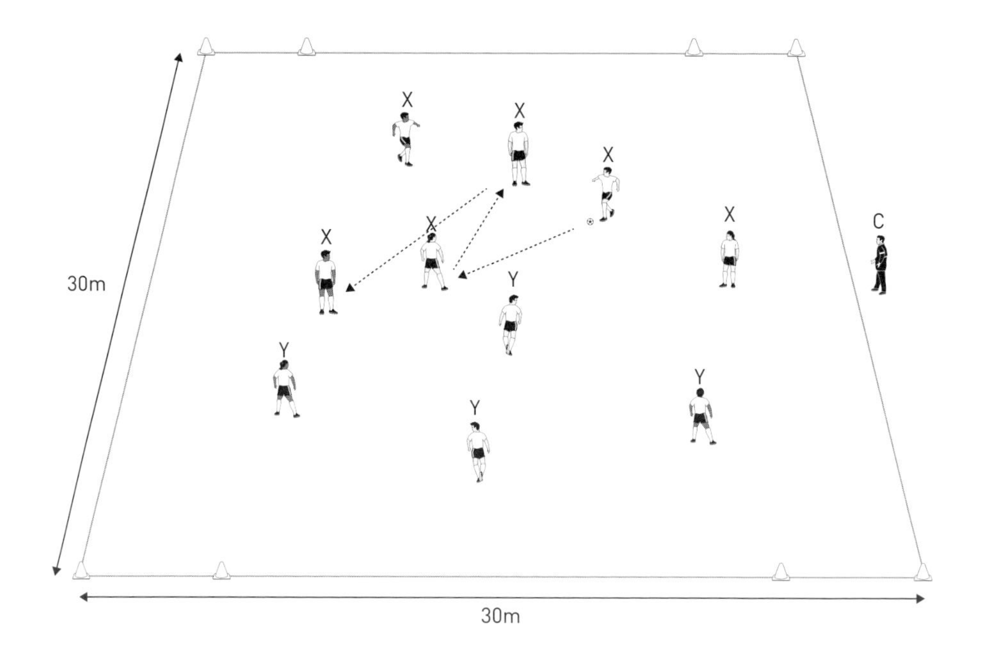

Organisation: Set out a 30 x 30m area with a small goal set up in each corner of the area using traffic cones. Organise the players into 6 v 4.

Equipment: Traffic cones, bibs, football.

Description: The teams play 6 v 4 inside the area. The objective for the team of six (X) is to keep possession. If the players make five passes in a row, they win one point. The objective for the team of four (Y) is to win the ball back and score through any of the four corner goals to score two points. The first team to 10 points is the winner.

Key coaching points: X team attempt to keep possession by creating space. Y team need to win the ball then quickly counter attack.

Progressions: X team may make a five passes then score into any of the corner goals for a bonus point. Limit players on X team to no more the two or three touches each time they receive the ball. Players on Y team may only score with a first-time finish.

>>> 47 – 49 – 64 – 72

session 96 1 v 1 to 4 v 4

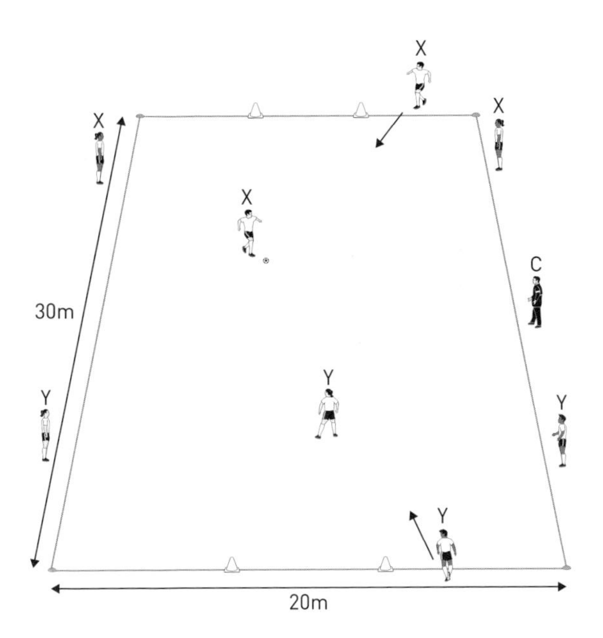

Organisation: Set out a 20 x 30m area with a small goal set up at each end of the area using traffic cones. Organise the players into two teams of 4 v 4.

Equipment: Marker cones, traffic cones, bibs, football.

Description: The first two players play 1 v 1 in the area. If a goal is scored, one point is scored and two players join the game to create a 2 v 2. If a goal is scored at 2 v 2, two points are scored and two more players join to make a 3 v 3. If a goal is score here, three points are scored and the final two players join to create a 4 v 4. In this final 4 v 4, a goal is worth four points. If the ball goes out of play at any stage – except when a goal is scored – the game resets with a 1 v 1 with two new starting players. Keep track of the score, and the first team to score 15 points wins.

Key coaching points: Keep possession and choose your attacks to ensure the ball doesn't go out of play. Help your teammates by moving to create space. Use your dribbling skills to beat the defender and open up an opportunity to score.

Progressions: Make the goals a little bigger and add goalkeepers to make it harder to score. Award bonus points for good skills and moves to beat a player (when up against a defender) to encourage attacking play. Award double points for a goal scored with the weaker foot.

››› 28 – 53 – 61 – 72

session 97 non-stop 3 v 3

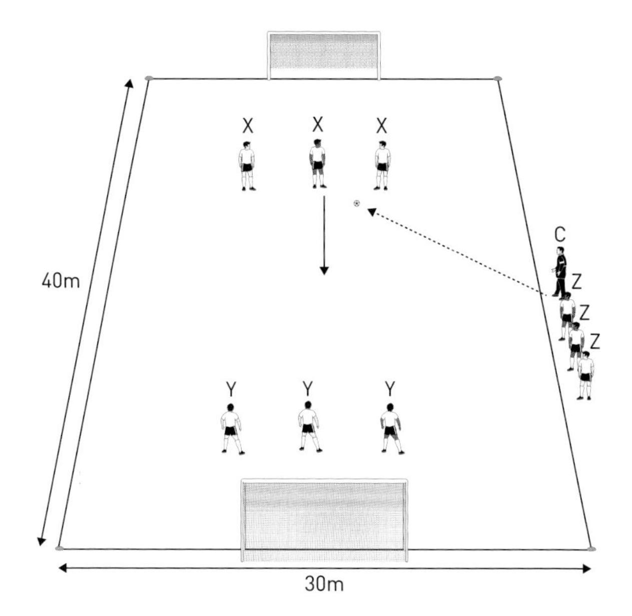

Organisation: Set out a 30 x 40m area with a goal at each end of the area. Organise the players into teams of three. Organise the teams so they are set up at each end of the area with one team resting to the side.

Equipment: Goals, marker cones, bibs, football.

Description: The coach passes a ball from the side of the area to one of the teams. They then attack the goal at the other end, while the players in the team at the other end attempt to stop them in a 3 v 3 small-sided game. As soon as that attack is over, the coach plays another ball in to the defending team, who then attack the goal at the other end against a new defending team of 3. Once a team has defended at one end they immediately become the attackers for the next 3 v 3 and so on. An attack is over once a goal is scored or has been successfully defended. The team that score the most goals are the winners.

Key coaching points: Be positive in attack, look to take the defenders on. Create space and shooting opportunities through movement. Defend as a team.

Progressions: Add goalkeepers to each goal to make it harder to score. Award bonus points for good skills and moves to beat a player (when up against a defender) to encourage attacking play. Award double points for a goal scored following more than three passes.

>>> 24 – 47 – 64 – 84

session 98 quick-fire soccer

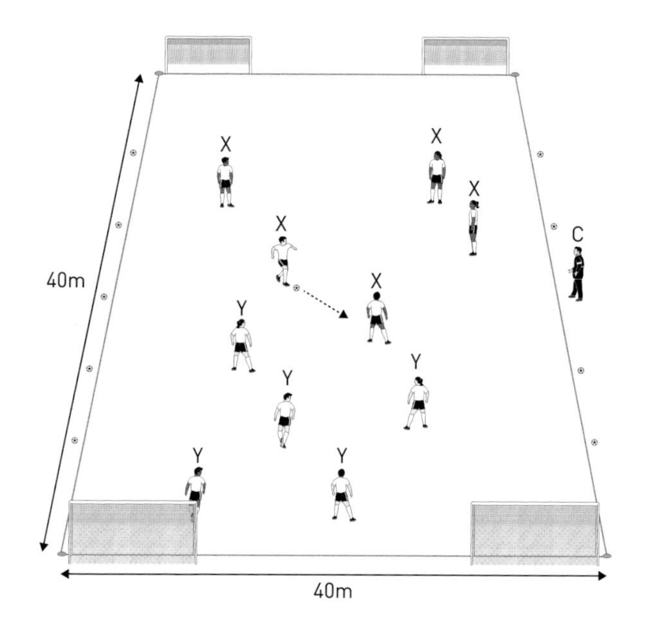

Organisation: Set out a 40 x 30m area with a four small goals, one placed in each corner. Organise the players into 5 v 5, and place five footballs spread along each touchline.

Equipment: Marker cones, bibs, footballs.

Description: The teams play 5 v 5 inside the area attempting to score into either of the opposition's two goals. As soon as a goal is scored or the ball goes out of play, the coach calls the name of a player who chooses any of the ten balls on the touchlines to continue the game, therefore constantly changing the start points of the game and angles of attack. Keep score and play until all ten balls have been used. This game is played without goalkeepers

Key coaching points: React quickly to the different positions of the restart. Look to switch play if one goal is covered. Defend as a team to protect your two goals.

Progressions: Add a goalkeeper to each goal to make it harder to score. Award double points for a goal scored following more than three passes. Limit players to a first-time finish only.

››› **23 – 54 – 66 – 87**

session 99 wing wizards

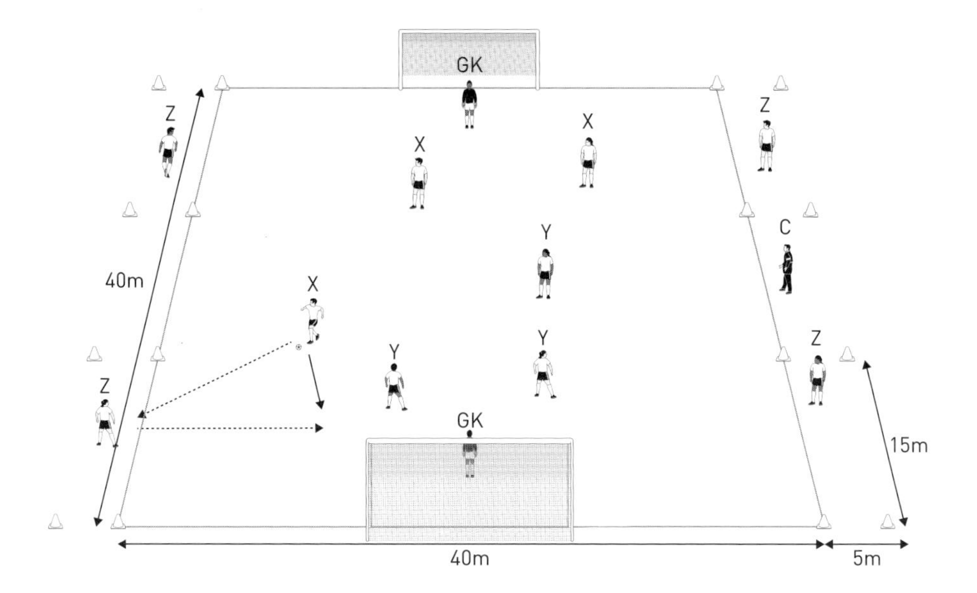

Organisation: Set out a 40 x 40m area with four 5 x 15m channels in each corner and a goal at each end. Organise players into 3 v 3 and place a goalkeeper (GK) in each of the goals. Add an extra four players, one in each of the wide channels.

Equipment: Goals, marker cones, traffic cones, bibs, football.

Description: The teams play 3 v 3 inside the central area attempting to score into the opposition's goal. In order to score a goal, the attacking team must play the ball out to any of the wide players, and then convert from the cross. The wide players play for both teams, and cross the ball for whichever team they received from.

Key coaching points: Make different runs to offer the wide player options for the cross and attack the ball from the cross. Look to switch play if one of the wide areas is covered. Defend as a team and track runners to prevent a goal being scored from the cross.

Progressions: Award double points for a goal scored following more than three passes. Limit players to a first-time finish only.

››› 40 – 50 – 70 – 85

session 100 5 v 5 in three goals

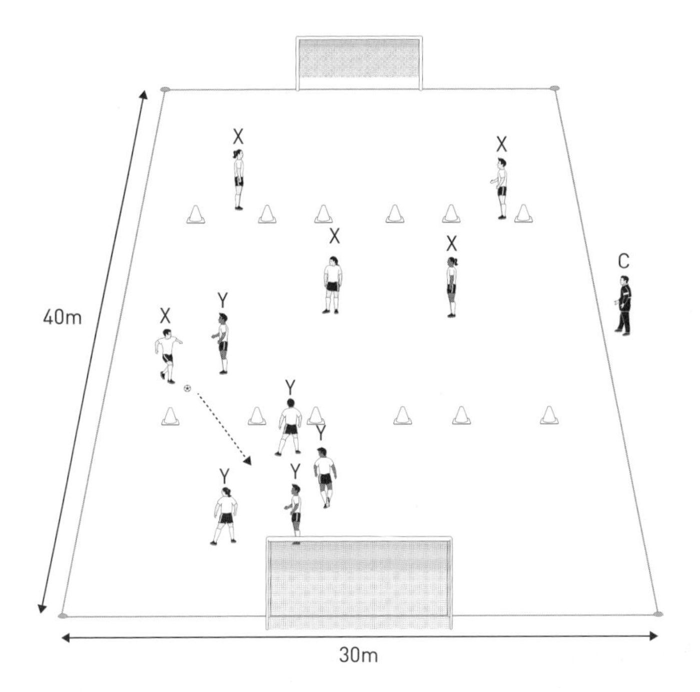

Organisation: Set out a 30 x 40m area. Two small goals are set up a short distance in front of each goal line, with a larger goal directly on the goal line at each end. Organise teams of 5 v 5.

Equipment: Goals, marker cones, traffic cones, bibs, football.

Description: The attackers try to dribble across one of the opposition's goal lines. They score one point for either central goal, and two points for the outer goal. Defenders surround the ball and pressure the attacker with the ball.

Key coaching points: X team attempt to keep possession by creating space. Y team need to win the ball by creating pressure and closing down space.

Progressions: Increase/decrease the size/number of goals. Overload the teams.

>>> 44 – 47 – 61 – 89

session 101 magic men

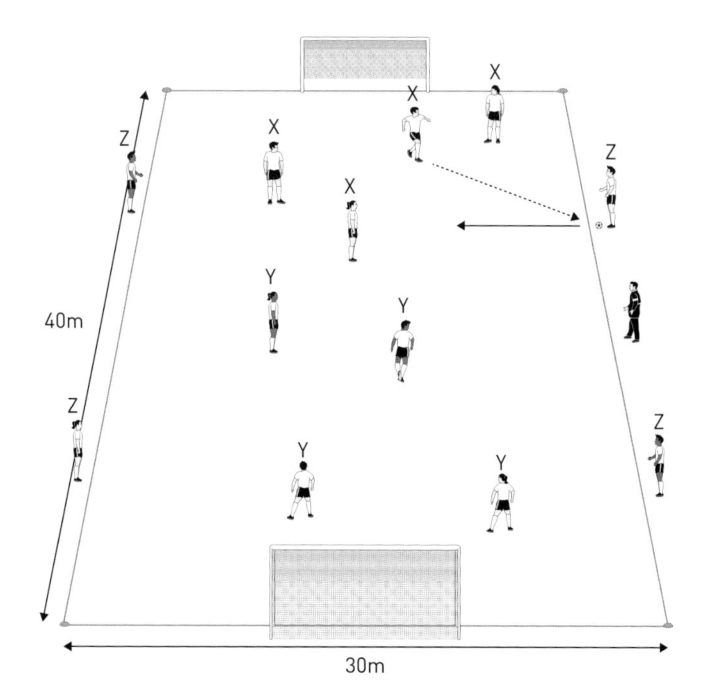

Organisation: Set out a 30 x 40m area with two goals. Organise players into three teams of four, with two teams (X and Y) playing and one team (Z) on the touchlines (two on each side) acting as magic men.

Equipment: Goals, marker cones, bibs, football.

Description: The teams play 4 v 4 in a normal game. The magic men (Z) positioned on the side are used as support players but are allowed to join in the main game once they have been passed to in order to create a 5 v 4 overload for the attacking team. Once the phase breaks down or the attacking team lose possession, the magic man returns to their spot on the sideline. Rotate teams so that all players have a chance to play in each role.

Key coaching points: Take advantage of your overload by keeping possession. Defend as a team when outnumbered.

Progressions: Magic men are not allowed to score, and must focus on support play. Magic men are limited to no more than three touches each time they receive the ball. Allow the teams to use a second magic man to create a 6 v 4 overload.

››› 48 – 60 – 64 – 76

SESSION PLANS

The following list of numbers relates to the sessions in the book and shows which games we feel work well together to make up one session. At the bottom of each page throughout the book we have matched each game with four others in order to create a full session of games and practices, which would last for a minimum of one hour. They are listed again here for you to use as a quick guide. Passing practices are linked to other passing games and small-sided games which are based around making passes, and subsequently the same applies for the sessions which focus on other techniques like dribbling, turning or shooting. This is simply a guide, so please feel free to mix and match the sessions to suit what you feel will most benefit your players and help them to get the most out of your sessions. As previously mentioned, the warm-ups tend to work well with all sessions as they are inclusive games based around movement and mobility.

GAME	No.	A	B	C	D
colour cone jumble	21	29	35	63	97
steal the ball	22	26	41	43	76
trio	23	32	54	64	99
danger squares	24	40	41	65	82
triple 1 v 1	25	28	40	61	89
dr. football	26	22	52	64	76
team pursuit	27	37	39	65	86
multi goal 1 v 1	28	25	30	41	96
turnover	29	21	35	39	82
keep ball 1-2-3	30	44	53	63	94
under the bridge	31	40	58	62	83
dribble, turn, pass, repeat	32	34	49	61	98
the fabulous five	33	35	36	45	83
colour corridors	34	32	56	57	84
figure of 8	35	33	38	65	86
sing soccer	36	45	43	64	86
turning circle	37	35	42	63	90
cone hunting	38	43	57	67	80
colour run	39	27	48	61	92
red square	40	31	53	65	90
end to end	41	24	57	64	97
football pinball	42	37	60	63	75
shark tank	43	38	53	68	96
goal-den gates	44	30	49	67	100
knights & dragons	45	36	40	61	90
weighted passes	46	49	59	61	101
pass point	47	49	51	68	82
two-touch tennis	48	28	60	70	84
target pass	49	37	44	46	85
chips	50	46	55	66	78
bounce ball	51	56	60	69	77
dodge it	52	26	56	62	81
3 v 1 to 1 v 1	53	41	48	61	75

GAME	No.	A	B	C	D
speedy strikers	54	32	53	63	100
the cube	55	48	56	70	95
minefield	56	55	47	63	73
magic ball	57	42	60	68	87
tunnel vision	58	31	56	62	71
happy hoops	59	46	54	66	94
2 v 1 passing target	60	32	57	64	99
speed demons	61	25	34	53	77
first-time finish	62	56	58	70	72
fast finish	63	37	41	49	89
countdown	64	40	60	69	90
goal crazy	65	28	42	63	91
shoot, head & volley	66	50	59	70	79
back to goal	67	33	58	62	93
shoot solo	68	25	52	61	80
shot race	69	53	54	64	88
two-touch finishing	70	48	50	66	81
corner cones	71	57	60	66	75
counter attack	72	40	53	64	90
attack v defence overload	73	48	58	69	95
tiki-taka	74	56	59	70	72
goals v targets	75	42	57	68	71
rugby football	76	30	53	66	101
corner ball	77	51	58	61	83
limited touch zones	78	35	48	48	91
diagonal goals	79	44	53	65	92
snookered	80	38	51	65	85
ten-pass total football	81	46	66	67	93
floating keepers	82	50	59	66	88
snooze soccer	83	28	53	61	77
3 v 3 cover your goal	84	44	60	68	97
quick-pass corners	85	55	60	70	83

(Continued)

GAME	No.	A	B	C	D
two zones	86	25	53	61	94
set piece soccer	87	50	56	66	98
over the wall	88	57	58	68	82
four goal 4 v 4	89	25	47	54	100
collect & attack	90	25	40	64	72
time team	91	47	64	68	81
man marking	92	22	24	61	79
centre goal	93	57	65	70	81
join the attack	94	30	52	69	86
goals v passes	95	47	49	64	72
1 v 1 to 4 v 4	96	28	53	61	72
non-stop 3 v 3	97	24	47	64	84
quick-fire soccer	98	23	54	66	87
wing wizards	99	40	50	70	85
5 v 5 in three goals	100	44	47	61	89
magic men	101	48	60	64	76